YOUR FAMILY HISTORY

YOUR FAMILY HISTORY

How to use oral history, personal family archives, and public documents to discover your heritage

BY

Allan J. Lichtman

VINTAGE BOOKS

A Division of Random House

NEW YORK

A VINTAGE ORIGINAL May 1978

FIRST EDITION

 Published in the United States by Random House, Inc., New York, and simultaneously in Canada by Random House of Canada Limited, Toronto.

Library of Congress Cataloging in Publication Data

Lichtman, Allan J
Your family history.
Bibliography: p.
Includes index.
1. Genealogy. 2. United States—Genealogy—Handbooks, manuals, etc. I. Title.
CS16.L53 929'.1'0202 77-76582
ISBN 0-394-72332-5

Manufactured in the United States of America

For my parents,

Gertrude and Emanuel Lichtman,

and my daughter Kara Martin Lichtman

ACKNOWLEDGMENTS

The work of my research assistants Lonnie Bunch and Gary Braithwaite, both graduate students at The American University, was important for all phases of the book, especially chapters 4 and 6. I am grateful to Esther M. Ridder for useful observations on interviewing technique, to Rodis Roth for guidance on material culture, to Joan Challinor for the chapter on family photographs, and to Bill Linder, Richard Lackey, and James Walker for their insights on genealogy. Thanks are also due Richard Breitman, Valerie French, Alan Kraut, Laura Irwin Langbein, Ronnie and Steven Lichtman, and Maris Vinovskis for comments on the manuscript, and Gail Winston, my editor at Random House, who has been helpful, patient, and understanding throughout the project. All errors and omissions, of course, I claim for myself.

CONTENTS

YOUR FAMILY HISTORY

Chapter 1

INTRODUCTION

WHEN I WAS A CHILD the family would sometimes linger at the table after a special dinner, eat ice cream from plastic soup bowls, and share stories about the "olden days." I remember the thrill of joining this adult group and listening to tales about the youth of my parents. For years, these few stories (retold many times), some casual remarks by relatives, and a handful of old photographs were my only sources of knowledge about my family's history. The depression years seemed to me an exciting time; my parents and their friends could go to the movies for a dime. Images of life during World War II came to me only through amusing stories of my father's soft duty as a radar technician in the Hawaiian Islands. Only later did I begin to understand my past, discovering a harsher side of family life and appreciating the real accomplishments of my ancestors. For the first time I learned about the genuine heroics of my immigrant grandparents and about their bitter disappointments. I realized that without consciously searching for family history, we are likely to have a dim and distorted vision of our own past.

In seeking the history of your family you experience the joys of discovering information long forgotten and the satisfaction of preserving memories that might otherwise be lost forever. As a family historian you re-create the lives of your ancestors. You unravel mysteries about your past, beginning to understand why family members act as they do, even how you came to be who you are. Doing family history brings you closer to parents, grandparents, children and other kin, while offering you a sense of continuity in a world of bewildering change.

The study of family history is not limited to genealogy. A genealogist concentrates on accurately reconstructing a person's line of descent by studying the relationship of one ancestor to another. Genealogy has flourished in recent years, becoming liberated from domination by those eager to find a trace of royalty in their bloodline or to prove their descent from patriots of the Revolutionary War. Rather than concentrating on finding notable ancestors, most genealogists now try to fill in as many branches of the family tree as possible. But doing a family history need not be restricted to the construction of a family tree. The family historian strives for a broader and more rewarding understanding of family life in the past and of the family's relations with the outside world. The family historian, more than the genealogist, relies on information gathered by talking to family members and by studying family heirlooms, letters, and photographs.

Today's family historians are not merely following a passing fad; they are taking part in a major redirection of historical study that began at the end of the 1950's. Once neglected almost entirely by historians, the family is now a major focus of their research. Traditionally, the history we learn in school or read about in textbooks is a parade of great men and women and of epochal events. This history centers around such imposing figures as Julius Caesar, Napoleon, Catherine the Great, and George Washington, and on notable incidents such as the fall of Rome, the signing of the Declaration of Independence, and the Battle of Gettysburg. Textbook history emphasizes the political sphere of life, focusing primarily on the struggle for power. However inspirational and important, this traditional history is remote from the experience of most Americans.

Historians have recently fashioned a "new history" that stresses the day-to-day experiences of ordinary people. The politics of the 1960's sensitized historians to the importance of studying women, children, poor people, and others who rarely were mentioned in traditional accounts of the past. They saw that they could enrich our understanding of history by recounting how most people lived and worked, by analyzing the options that were open to them, and by finding out what values and expectations they shared. Historians also took a fresh approach to historical change, portraying human events as moving from the bottom up rather than from the top down. No longer were the common folk seen only as those who endured the deeds and misdeeds of history's movers and shakers. In the words of Gertrude Himmelfarb, "The victims of history have become its principal agents and actors."

For these "new historians," the family is a natural object of study. Humanity's most fundamental and most durable institution, the family has been responsible for producing and nuturing children, for molding the values of individuals, and for transmitting culture from one generation to the next. It provides love and emotional support for both children and adults, and arranges the daily lives of its members. The study of families can illuminate the workings of an entire society, revealing details of people's movement from place to place, of opportunities for social and economic advancement, of relationships between the sexes. Changes in the nature of family life, historians believe, both influence and are influenced by social, economic, and political change.

Historians of the family have drawn upon new methods of research, often borrowed from other disciplines, that enable them to re-create the lives of families that are not represented in such traditional records as letters, diaries, and diplomatic dispatches. Using the techniques of demographers, for example, historians have constructed from marriage contracts, tax lists, census reports, baptismal certificates, and death records, statistical portraits of anonymous families that include details like family size and composition, ages at marriage, births, and deaths. Touched by the scholar's hand, households are restored to life, revealing family structures for periods before accurate national statistics were collected.

Historians have combined statistical and psychological approaches to history.As John Demos has noted, "quantitative information . . . provides us—if all goes well —with certain concrete bench-marks: age of weaning, age of marriage, rate of mortality and so forth. . . . Psychological theory cries out for solid evidence on the timing of certain crucial 'life-happenings.'" Demos's own work seeks to bridge the divide between the circumstances and the psychology of family life. In *A Little Commonwealth: Family Life in Plymouth Colony,* Demos applies the psychological theories of Erik Erikson to patterns of child-rearing in seventeenth-century Plymouth. Drawing on both statistical and literary sources, Demos describes early childhood in this Puritan colony as marked by "a year of general indulgence" followed by a "radical turn towards severe discipline," especially by parental efforts to crush the child's earliest efforts at self-assertion. According to Demos, Erikson's model of human development suggests that if a child's struggles to achieve autonomy, to "stand on his own feet," are beaten down rather than supported, a preoccupation with shame and guilt can be expected later in life. Thus Demos concludes that distinctive patterns for the rearing of children explain why shame, guilt, and the struggle to save face loom so large in Puritan culture.

Reflecting the new emphasis on families, historical studies have begun to show the folly of deducing from our knowledge of the present what family life in the past must have been like. A famous example of the dangers of backward projection is the Moynihan report on the black family, submitted to President Johnson in 1965 by Daniel Patrick Moynihan, currently a senator from New York State. Without actually studying the history of black families, Moynihan conjectured that the slavery experience had destroyed black people's commitment to family life and their ability to maintain stable families. This historical experience, Moynihan argued, was largely responsible for the "tangle of pathology" that he claimed characterized black families of his own time. Yet study after study of actual history has shown that despite slavery black people remained committed to family life, and that stable two-parent families predominated in the period immediately following emancipation.

As a family historian you gain a richer understanding of your past than can be achieved through genealogy alone. And you uncover aspects of the past that can't be found in history books alone. Historians necessarily offer generalizations about the experiences of large numbers of people and many families; you will be exploring the lives of your own ancestors and the families they formed. Some of your forebears will seem to have stepped out of a history book; others will confound and contradict the conclusions of professional historians.

A project in family history can be as modest or as ambitious as you choose. You need not acquire years of special training or devote a decade of your life to finding your roots. Although full-scale investigations can be especially satisfying, you can still learn much about your heritage without beginning a major study. Try chatting informally with family members about incidents in their lives and their memories of other kin. Start collecting family documents, heirlooms, and photographs, or write for records about your more distant ancestors. Or begin your autobiography. Any project, no matter how small, will be rewarding.

Family history is neither a contest to find the relative most remote in time nor a search for illustrious ancestors. Those who explore their history are often amazed at what they gain by simply going back two generations. Just two generations include six direct ancestors, each with a story to tell, and at least three family groups, each with a history of its own. One more generation adds another eight ancestors and at least four more families.

One student told me that the first time she ever really talked to her grandfather and found out what he was like was when she interviewed him for a class project. Through hearing about his life, she found it possible to empathize with what she had once dismissed as the odd habits of an old man. Only after hearing stories about his upbringing in an Arkansas orphanage did she begin to comprehend why he still felt uncomfortable in company and often went off to read by himself at family gatherings.

I learned that at the age of eighteen my own grandmother had come to the United States from Poland. Not speaking a word of English, she worked as a seamstress in the sweatshops of New York's garment center, eventually saving enough money to send for her parents, her two sisters, and her three brothers. Prohibition, which I knew about from books and movies, came alive for me when I heard about the gin her family made in the bathtub. They once pulled the plug and dashed out the back door when federal agents came to their front door. The G-men, it seems, did not concentrate just on the breweries of Dutch Shultz and Al Capone.

A Bostonian in his fifties recently traveled for the first time to his mother's birthplace in Montana. In a small town he discovered the house she lived in as a child; everything was exactly as she had once described it. Without telling her, he slipped some pictures of the house into the packet of photographs he was showing her from the trip. Suddenly she exclaimed, "That's my house!" After seventy years in the East, she still recognized it immediately. And it was still "my house," not "the house where I once lived." The photographs of the house brought forth memories and stories about small-town life in Montana at the turn of the twentieth century.

As a family historian you can make trends of the contemporary world work for you. As our life spans have increased, so has the likelihood that kinfolk from several generations will be alive at the same time. The telephone, the postal service, the airplane, and the automobile make it possible to locate and communicate with family members regardless of where they live. Modern record-keeping can also help you document your family's past. No matter what your ethnic origin, no matter how recent your lineage in America, you should not assume that the more distant past of your family is lost forever. The children and grandchildren of immigrants have followed their family through several generations of Old World history, and black Americans have found traces of their ancestry in records dating from before the Civil War.

Family history, though, does not begin in the past; it begins with questions of personal identity. Who am I? Where did I come from? How did I get to be as I am? Where am I headed? These are the questions that lead you into a quest for your heritage.

In other times and places, answers to the riddles of identity were woven into the fabric of an ongoing traditional culture. For those living in a traditional society, mythology or religion adequately explained the world. People often lived where their ancestors had lived for generations and where they expected their children to live. They were surrounded by kinfolk and others who shared their values and outlook on life. The tasks a person performed and the skills he or she possessed were themselves probably part of a family heritage. Work was not sharply separated from home life, as folk labored at home or near home, often with family members and other relatives. Institutions such as the church and the government were personal presences in the community. Ordinary folk did not expect things to change very much in their lifetime or in that of their children. Traditional societies of the ancient world, for instance, viewed time as a snake bent into a circle, swallowing its own tail. The same basic events that began the world circled endlessly with no important changes.

Men and women of modern society, however, may find that answers to the elemental mysteries of life, including those of personal identity, seem more elusive. Many of us in the Western world still cherish traditional values and ways of life. And advances in the struggle against death, disease, poverty, and despotism have both liberated us and in some respects made our lives more orderly and predictable. But modern life may also bring with it a special kind of loneliness and isolation. We no longer share a single unified view of the world; our vision is broken into pieces by the differing perspectives of religion, science, and common sense. We usually work away from our homes and have little sense that our tasks are sanctioned by tradition. Most of us expect to change our place of residence several times during our lives and anticipate that our children will leave home and enjoy their own lives elsewhere. Few of us have access to the sources of power within our society; the corporation and the government seem remote from individual people, difficult to understand, and impossible to control. Rather than stability, we expect to experience continual, often unpredictable change. Some historians have even speculated that life in the Western world has changed more radically during the last hundred years than in all its previous history.

The poet Percy Bysshe Shelley expressed the plight of modern man when he wrote that we "look before and after and pine for what is not." To understand ourselves today we need a vision of our past. We long to find out who our ancestors were, where they once lived, and why they left and came to a new world. The noted anthropologist David Schneider recently told a national symposium on kin and communities that "the most rootless yearn for roots; the most mobile bemoan their placeless fate; the most isolated yearn for kin and community, for these represent the basic things that make life worth living for many people."

Family history is the one unifying thread that runs through everyone's life. If all else seems to be in flux, your family heritage remains the same. No matter what you do in life, your family history belongs uniquely to you, yet makes you part of a tradition that goes beyond yourself and your own time. You can ignore your roots or even try to renounce them, but you can never change or destroy them. Alex Haley captured the nation's attention with the triumphant story of one man's family. *Roots,* it seems, struck closer to home than any pure fiction or general history. For some of us, however, admiration may have been mingled with a touch of guilt about how little we know of our own roots.

Modern psychology now recognizes that learning about our past vastly improves our understanding of ourselves. We as individuals cannot be isolated from either the present or past generations of our family. Families, it seems, transmit across many generations values, expectations, even sentiments and emotions. A fear of falling short of expectations or a feeling that family problems are your own fault can be passed on in a family as surely as brown hair, high cheekbones, and broad shoulders.

Psychiatrists in clinical practice have suggested that the person who understands the patterns of thinking and feeling that emerge over generations of family history is likely to function better as a secure, responsible, self-directed person. As part of their psychiatric training at Georgetown University Medical School, many students of

Dr. Murray Bowen, a pioneer in family therapy and himself a family historian, have explored their own family histories. After many years of working with families, Dr. Bowen observed that "it became increasingly impossible to see a single person without seeing his total family sitting like phantoms alongside him." Although Thomas Wolfe may have correctly noted that you can't go home again, each of us takes a large chunk of home along with us wherever we go.

The Pueblo Indians of America's Southwest have an age-old tradition that unites individuals with their forebears. Pueblo villagers in a region of New Mexico can follow trails that lead from their separate communities to an ancient shrine high in the mountains. The travelers know that for centuries before them, their ancestors followed the same trail and performed the same ceremony. They know that someday their own descendants will make the same journey, maintaining spiritual unity from one generation to the next. Most of us cannot journey along mountain trails that lead to communion with our ancestors. But we can travel through time, rescuing our ancestors from oblivion and ourselves from isolation. Family history is a journey of discovery. What you discover is your own heritage and a part of the collective heritage shared by all human beings.

This guide begins with a brief introduction to your richest and most accessible source of information, the history recorded in your own memory and in the memories of your close relatives. It then suggests the kinds of questions that can take you beyond genealogy to explorations of how people lived in the past, of what they thought and felt, of how the history of their times touched their personal lives. After the techniques necessary for exploiting the oral histories of family members are laid out in detail, other chapters lead you through sources available in the home, disclosing what can be learned from family heirlooms, documents, and photographs. Later chapters discuss how to locate and use both published and unpublished materials in libraries, archives, and other repositories. The final chapter explains how to plan, organize, and present your research. The best way to use this guide is to read it from beginning to end before starting your research. Then once you get involved in your project you can return to specific sections of the book for additional guidance on particular matters of interest.

Chapter 2

BEGINNING FAMILY HISTORY: WHAT TO ASK

THE BEST WAY to start family history is to explore your own memories and talk to close family members. You need not journey to a distant library and putter around dusty archives to begin gaining insight into your personal heritage. Use your most precious resource, people's memories, and become the oral historian of your family.

Oral history is an exciting and productive form of research that elicits and records people's recollections of their experiences, thoughts, and feelings. Our memories go beyond names, dates, and places to fill the past with people's struggles and accomplishments in times very different from our own. Although we usually take pains to bequeath material resources to our survivors, oddly we neglect the even more valuable resources locked in our thoughts and memories.

As an oral historian of your family you will forge new relationships with family members while enabling them to leave future generations the legacy of their own ideas and experiences. Parents, grandparents, children, aunts, uncles, cousins, brothers, sisters, and friends of the family are repositories of information and insights that can be obtained from no other source. Oral history will tell you something about virtually any aspect of family history that might be of interest to you. In most cases, conversations with people will help you learn about four or even five generations of a family.

The effort to ransack your own memory and chat informally with close relatives is an exploratory stage of research that will help you plan a more ambitious program for studying family history. Later, you will want to talk to your relatives again, conducting a more formal interview and using information acquired from other sources. This chapter will introduce you to oral history and to the questions that can guide your thinking and research. The following chapter will discuss specific oral-history techniques.

Increasingly, professional historians are coming to appreciate the value of tapping people's memories. Although oral history is not new, it has been reborn in our own time. More than four centuries before the birth of Christ, Herodotus, generally regarded as the father of history, used oral testimony for his account of the war between the Greeks and the Persians. Although modern historians turned away from oral evidence and emphasized research into written documents, oral history has now regained respectability as a vital supplement to documentary research. No longer wedded to the written word, today's historians appreciate what can be learned from material objects, photographs, movies, and oral testimony.

Recent interest in oral history has resulted in new efforts to interview society's leaders—Supreme Court justices, senators, corporation presidents, Nobel laureates, as well as their friends and colleagues. Such interviews offer the historian unique information while enabling individuals to relate aspects of events that can't be found in the written record. These interviews provide insight into the biographies of notable people, help scholars understand how significant decisions were reached, clarify events hidden from public view, and illuminate the workings of such institutions as legislatures, courts, and corporations.

Historians are also interested in the oral histories of ordinary Americans. They have used interviews to trace changes in the lives of individuals and families and to explore the distinctive cultures of occupational, ethnic, and religious groups within the United States. Historians have also begun encouraging Americans to draw out the oral histories of family members and contribute their results to scholarly research. For example, the Anonymous Family History Project, co-sponsored by the Department of History at Clark University and the Social Welfare Archives at the University of Minnesota, is designed to assist students with the preparation of personal family histories and to provide facilities for the collection and storage of these studies.

If oral history is a good starting point for people beginning family history, it should not become your only route to the past. Interviews with relatives can be integrated with research into family documents, material objects, and sources located in libraries and archives. Each approach to your past can supply fresh information as well as a means of cross-checking what you have learned from your other research. Studying your family history is like putting together a jigsaw puzzle. You get bits and pieces of information that mean little by themselves, but can be fitted together to form a coherent picture of the past. Yet the family historian doesn't work with a constant number of pieces or with advance knowledge of what the picture should look like. Each source supplies new pieces that not only fill in blank spaces but also change or expand the scene itself. Since family history is limitless in scope, the portion of the puzzle that you work on is determined by the questions that you ask about the past. Before interviewing a single person you should think about what you want to find out.

QUESTIONS FOR FAMILY HISTORY

"What is the answer?" the dying novelist Gertrude Stein asked Alice B. Toklas, her lifelong friend. Hearing no reply, Stein asked again, "In that case, what is the question?" To begin studying your family history you should have some idea of what kinds of questions you want to ask. These questions can be quite broad and general when you first begin. As you gain knowledge and experience your inquiry may become much more specific.

There are a vast number of questions that you can begin exploring with members of your family. By thinking beforehand about what you want to learn, you give directon and coherence to your research. But you should also be alert to new avenues of inquiry opened by unexpected information or simply by greater familiarity with the history of your family.

You should pose research questions with a thought to gaining more than snapshots of family life. Try to see how life within the family changes over time. Change can take place both within the course of a family's life cycle and from one generation to the next. Your father's family may be quite different in many respects from the family of his father. But aspects of your father's family may have changed profoundly from the time when he first married to the time when his children left home and he retired from business. Questions you find interesting can be applied to people from different generations and to the same person at different periods of his life.

Of course, since I don't know your family I can't tell you what specific questions to pursue in family history research. But I can indicate important categories of questions, and within each category I can offer examples of concrete issues that you can explore.

THE FAMILY TREE

Even the family historian who plans a broad research program would probably want to ask the basic questions of genealogy. Who were my ancestors? Where and when were they born? Where did they die? What was their relationship to one another? In answering these questions you construct what genealogists term a family pedigree, which is more commonly known as a family tree. Genealogists have fashioned charts to help you record these answers and simultaneously visualize your own line of descent. Each of these types of charts reveals a different level of insight into the crisscross of affiliations that is your historical family. First, charts portraying your basic family tree (see Figure 1) include only your direct ancestors—parents, grandparents, great-grandparents, and so forth—and have space for the dates (and sometimes places) of birth, death, and marriage. Visually this chart looks like a tree with ever-widening branches. Beginning with you at the very bottom, each ascending level includes a greater number of ancestors. By the time the chart reaches your great-great-grandparents it already includes 30 direct ancestors; two generations later it will include 126 direct

ANCESTOR CHARTS

Figure 1: Basic Family Tree

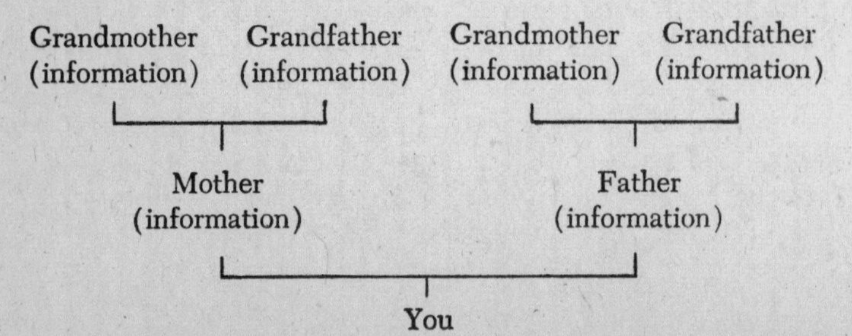

ancestors. Working with this simple type of chart you will be amazed at how much information you can fill in from your own knowledge and that of other family members. One of the most exciting experiences of family history is to watch your family tree first begin to take shape.

More complex types of genealogical charts list kinfolk other than direct ancestors in each generation of your family history. One chart, sometimes called a descendant's chart (see Figure 2), includes the brothers and sisters of each of your forebears (your aunts and uncles) as well as the people they marry. Another even more complicated

Figure 2: Descendant's Chart

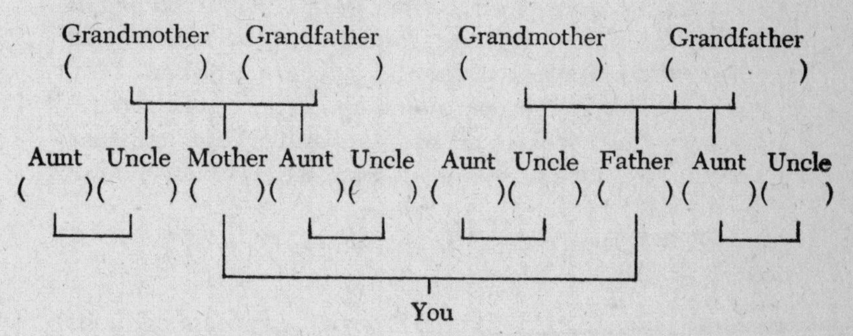

Figure 3: Collateral Kin Chart

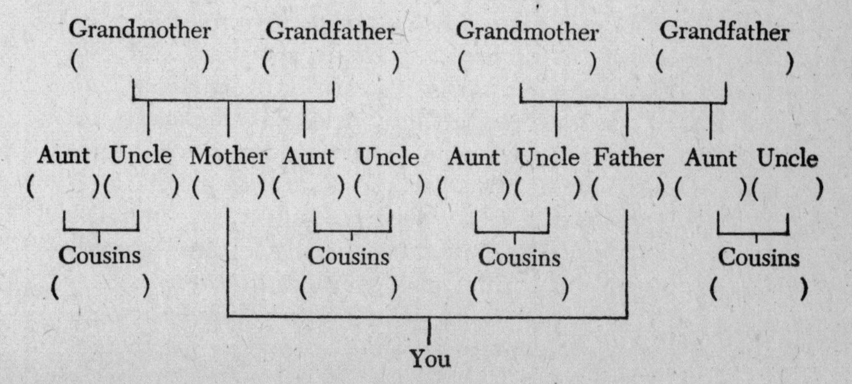

chart, sometimes called a collateral kin chart (see Figure 3), includes the children of your aunts and uncles in each generation (your cousins) and perhaps even the people they marry (your cousins by marriage).

You can purchase genealogical charts or make them yourself; once you understand the format of a chart, you simply duplicate the same pattern for each generation. You may also devise a numbering system to identify different types of kin. Standard works on genealogy (see Chapter 6) describe various numbering systems and discuss their pros and cons. If you use genealogical charts, you will quickly begin to see how widely your heritage extends. Genealogists working on their own family history often find that they are related to other genealogists who began with seemingly separate ancestry. Journalist and genealogy buff Dan Rottenberg has described how genealogy reveals our common humanity. "It teaches us," he wrote, "that we are all brothers and sisters, and that whatever harm we do to one another, we do to ourselves."

THE STRUCTURE AND DYNAMICS OF FAMILY LIFE

Beyond genealogy, a family historian can explore both the structure and the inner workings of his ancestors' families. Since the publication in 1960 of Philippe Ariès's work *Centuries of Childhood: A Social History of Family Life,* attempts to understand family structure and dynamics have been a priority concern of professional historians. In this now classic study, Ariès linked changes in family life to the evolution of the modern world and challenged long-cherished notions about the meaning of modernity. Surveying the Western family from medieval times through the Industrial Revolution, he disputed the views of historians who pointed to the decline of the family during these years. Ariès claimed instead that the family triumphed in the modern era, exercising far greater power and influence than in earlier ages. In the Middle Ages, Ariès contended, the family was not a distinct unit separated from the rest of society, and roles within the family were not sharply defined. He argued that children mingled freely with adults, and family members with the rest of society. In his view, people felt no need for family privacy; they perceived no gulf between the world of the family and the domain of outsiders, or between the sphere of the adult and that of the child. Only in the sixteenth and seventeenth centuries, Ariès maintained, did the family begin to turn inward and recognize the need for educating children, for sheltering and preparing them for the transition to adult life. These changes, he insisted, tightened the emotional bonds between family members, separated people from the broader society, increased suspicion of those outside the family, and made the family a central institution for maintaining order and discipline.

A major project of family historians is simply to learn the size and composition of households. The issue of family size and composition has even become part of the current debate over family life, as critics of today's families bemoan the loss of support and security supposedly provided by the once-prevalent extended family of parents, children, grandparents, and other relatives. Consistent with Ariès's thesis of the increasing isolation of the family, many scholars have argued that industrialization led to the dissolution of the extended family and the rise of a nuclear family (parents and children). But studies by historians now suggest that the nuclear family was the norm throughout American history. People seem to have established separate households as a matter of choice and to have expanded the family largely out of necessity rather than preference. At different stages in the life cycle of a family, different people may temporarily have resided within the household. Yet research does indicate that households are generally smaller today and couples are more likely to live together without marrying or having children. Before the twentieth century, however, families were much more likely to include such outsiders as boarders, lodgers, and servants.

As a family historian you might want to determine how many people of various kinds lived in the households of your ancestors at different periods of time. The following checklist indicates possible residents:

1. father
2. mother
3. son
4. daughter
5. grandparent
6. aunt
7. uncle
8. cousin
9. friend
10. household help
11. boarder or lodger
12. other nonrelative

Knowledge about the size and composition of a household is significant in itself and can supply clues about the circumstances people faced and the nature of life within the family. The presence of servants or boarders can indicate something about the economic status of a family. Comparison between the numbers of children and the number and size of rooms in a residence may tell you something about family privacy. Psychiatrists have found that the number of brothers and sisters a person has and his or her place in the birth order can have an important influence on personality. Most authorities would likewise agree that growing up in an extended family may be very different from growing up in a nuclear family.

Historians realize, however, that the household as a place of residence is not the same as a family, a group of people tied together by emotional bonds and by close association with one another. Some historians, for example, have claimed that although the type of kin usually residing in American households may not have changed substantially, in the past, Americans were generally closer to kinfolk living in other households.

Recent work suggests that in some situations families may not be residentially based at all, and may depend only in part on biological relationships. As Carol B. Stack has shown in *All Our Kin,* a sensitive study of a poor black community called The Flats, people may adapt to circumstance by forming kin groups that are diffused over several households and aren't necessarily related by blood. Families in The Flats were flexible groups united primarily by the need for mutual aid. As Stack has written:

> Without the help of kin, fluctuations in the meager flow of available goods could easily destroy a family's ability to survive. Kin and close friends who fall into similar economic crises know that they may share the food, dwelling, and even the few scarce luxuries of those individuals in their kin network. Despite the relatively high cost of rent and food in urban black communities, the collective power within kin-based exchange networks keeps people from going hungry.

The families in The Flats cannot properly be understood by looking at household composition and genealogical relationships. Neither can these families be classified into such conventional categories as nuclear, extended, or matriarchal families. Households in The Flats regularly were formed and dissolved, expanded and contracted. Adults transferred children from one residence to another, and domestic tasks were shared by all. A person's family consisted of both relatives and fictive kin, friends who assumed the rights and obligations of kin, were treated as kin by family members, and were even called by such kinship terms as sister, aunt, and uncle. Parental roles were not necessarily assumed by the biological mother and father, but by various mothers and fathers at different times, each of whom had specific rights and responsibilities. One parent might be in charge of discipline, another in charge of educational training, and yet another in charge of curing illness.

Key members of a cooperating kin group may remain invisible to the family historian who limits the family to the household and fails to recognize the flexibility of conventional family roles. Thus sociologists who diagnose the contemporary black family as caught in the "pathology" of "female-headed households" have failed to see that men may still be members of the kin group, performing many of the roles usually associated with fatherhood. When looking into your own history stay alert to the different forms of family life people may develop in response to individual circumstances.

Even if you can establish that families in your past were household-based and that parents assumed conventional roles, a great many questions are still relevant to understanding relationships among kinfolk. For instance, did kinfolk live near each other, work at the same jobs, possess the same skills, engage in joint business ventures, hold land in common, lend money and goods to each other, migrate to the same places? How often did relatives visit, write, or speak with one another? Did relatives share such services as babysitting and care for the sick and destitute? What was expected in return for a service or for financial assistance? What was the relationship between genealogical position and family roles? Did the family recognize fictive kin? Did family groups gather together for holidays like Christmas and Thanksgiving? Did kinfolk hold reunions or similar types of family gatherings? Was there a family club? What happened to widows, orphans, and widowers?

You can learn a lot about family dynamics by studying everyday events. *Losing Battles,* Eudora Welty's magnificent novel about life in the South, centers around the Beecham family reunion in Banner, Mississippi, and offers great insight into the meaning and practice of kinship. One memorable scene shows the importance of family ties for people of rural Mississippi. Family stories told at the reunion and an old post card produced from between the pages of the family Bible seem to show that Gloria Renfro, wife of a Beecham grandson, was herself a descendant of the Beechams. "I don't want to be a Beecham! . . . I won't be a Beecham," Gloria cries as the Beecham women pin her to the ground, forcing watermelon down her throat and trying to make her "Say Beecham!" "Can't you say Beecham?" they taunt her. "What's wrong with being Beecham." "Let's make her say Beecham! *We* did!"

In your own study of a family reunion you might inquire about attendance, scheduling, location, financing, and naming. The Beecham family reunion included descendants and married kin of "Granny" Elvira Jordan Renfro, the central figure of the reunion. The gathering was held every year on her birthday, at the home built by her grandfather. Relatives came from Banner and neighboring towns, and one, Uncle Nathan, from parts unknown. Did your family hold formal reunions, or did less formal gatherings serve a similar purpose? Who was eligible to attend the family reunion? How regularly did people attend? How were they notified? How far did people travel? What pressures were exerted for attendance? How did attendance change over time? Could those attending bring nonrelatives? Why did people attend? Where was the reunion held? How regularly and how often was it held? Who paid for food and other costs? What name did family members have for the gathering?

You will also want to look at what happened at a reunion and what people thought of the occasion. The Beechams served mountains of food at an outdoors table —chicken pie from newly killed hens, homemade sausage, home-cured ham, pickled peaches, buttermilk, freshly baked cakes, enormous watermelons. The gathered relatives venerated the family Bible and listened to a sermon and a recitation of family history. They gave out awards to the oldest, the youngest, the most recent bride, the thinnest, the fattest, and the grandchild with the most descendants. Children played baseball, and adults sat and talked about family and local history. The reunion ended when all joined hands, sang "Blest Be the Tie," and listened to a final benediction. What types of food were served at your family reunion? Did objects like a family Bible play a role in the gathering? Were ceremonies performed that centered around certain activities or elderly relatives? What types of games were played? Were prizes and awards handed out? What type of family business was transacted? What did people talk about? Were religious observances part of the reunion? Were activities and family business segregated by sex? Were children separated from adults? What did people like and dislike about reunions? How did reunions change over time? If a previous practice of holding reunions was ended, why was this step taken?

By asking these questions about family reunions you can better understand what binds kinfold together and what relatives hope to achieve by meeting with each other. Such knowledge can indicate who exercises power and responsibility and how kinfolk regard fictive kin or relatives by marriage as compared to blood relations. It can suggest how closely people identify with their kin, how people organize themselves into family groups, and which of their many lines of descent people consider most significant. Knowledge about reunions can also disclose how tasks and authority are divided between men and women, how children fit into a kin group, and how members of different generations view their kinship affiliations.

Beyond inquiring about kinship, you can look into many other topics relevant to what goes on in a family. Here are some suggested ways of looking at the family that can help you channel your research. Consider how the family arranges the daily lives of individuals. Decisions made within a family often determine where a person lives, how he spends his time, and what opportunities and options are open to him. Should the family move to another town to take advantage of better employment or educational opportunities for a family member? How is the money in the family budget allocated? What household tasks do family members perform? What rules are imposed on children of various ages? How much time do family members spend with each other? What do they do together and separately? How do family members spend their leisure time? Do children work or go to school? Remember that in the past, child labor was much more prevalent than it is today. Which adults within the family work outside the home? Don't assume that in the past, men always worked and women always stayed home. This was not true for many frontier families, for colonial families engaged in home industry, or for nineteenth-century families whose young women worked in the textile mills of New England. And it was not true for the Orthodox Jewish family of my great-grandparents. My great-grandmother ran the family business, while my great-grandfather devoted himself to study and prayer.

The family historian should pay attention to the decision-making process in the family. How did sex roles affect the exercise of power within the family? Did the father dominate the family? Did it seem that the father held sway, while the mother actually manipulated things behind the scenes? Did children have a say in family decisions? Did men and women have distinct spheres of authority and responsibility? Did males or females control family earnings and property? Laws in nineteenth-century America, for instance, gave husbands control over a wife's earnings and property. Studies of the twentieth century, however, show that women often control the family purse strings. (My father used to say that he controlled important matters like the family's position on national issues, while my mother controlled trivial things like how money should be spent.)

You can view the family as an organization with definite means of exit and entry. Sociologists tell us that we usually have two families: the family into which we are born or adopted and the family that we voluntarily form. Pivotal moments in our lives are when we leave our first family and when we start another family of our own. Sometimes these two events occur simultaneously; sometimes one precedes the other. In addition, through divorce or desertion, people voluntarily break up families and begin new ones. Obviously death may also shatter a family. For the families of your own past you might want to determine the ages at which people left their parents' home and the ages at which they married. Available evidence suggests that in earlier times people both left home and married later than they do today. Parents could better control children that stayed at home and could tap their valuable labor. You might also want to study the incidence of divorce, desertion, death, and remarriage. Although divorce is more prevalent today, it seems that desertion as well as death was more prevalent in the past.

Yet other questions advance an understanding of how families form and dissolve. What courtship and marriage practices did people follow? Did families use matchmakers? Did dating mean an intention to marry? What did people do on dates? What ceremonies were performed when children left home, or when people married, had children, or died? Did families have dowries for their daughters? Did they hold large weddings to which the whole community was invited? Did they have wakes or sit shivah when people died? What were funerals like? Why did people leave home at certain times or marry when they did? How were divorced and widowed people treated? Did family planning take place? How was it carried out? How were estates divided among potential heirs?

You can also look at the family in terms of its basic functions. It provides emotional support, privacy, love, and affection for individuals. It produces and raises children and teaches them values and skills. The family performs economic tasks and cares for the sick, the displaced, the elderly, the destitute, and the insane. The study of any one function could be an entire project in itself. In looking at privacy, for example, you would want to learn how different people defined privacy and what value privacy had for them. You would want to determine what were considered private and public spheres of life. You would want to examine the number of people in a household, the size of the residence, the number of rooms, the functions of each room (particularly in the past, rooms often had multiple functions), the sleeping and living arrangements. You would want to explore the family's access to transportation, the availability of private places nearby, the extent to which family members, other relatives, friends, and neighbors pried into one another's affairs. And you would want to discover how individuals and agencies outside the family—social workers, clergymen, police, creditors, employers, employees—affected the privacy of family members. In considering care of the sick you might want to find out who in the family had responsibility for such care. You might want to study the home remedies used by families, sources of medical advice, and the separation of the sick from the rest of the family. You might want to investigate how the family defined physical and mental illness, whether they had a private doctor, and how they financed health care. And you might want to probe the family's reliance on such institutions as the hospital or the asylum.

In addition, you can study the family as a web of close emotional relationships. Psychiatrists and psychologists believe that what happens to us within our family, particularly during the early years of life, shapes our personalities and values. Most of us, of course, are not competent to analyze the intimate psychology of family life; indeed, the experts themselves cannot agree about how best to understand the psychology of human beings. Freudians, Jungians, Skinnerians, Gestaltists, and advocates of many other psychological schools offer a bewildering variety of conflicting theories. Without becoming a theorist of any kind, however, you can begin to explore the emotional life of families in your past. As I mentioned earlier, behavior patterns, attitudes, and beliefs often recur over several generations of family history. You can search for such patterns and try to figure out their significance. In his study of the illustrious Adams family of New England, David Musto found that the family imposed on each generation of male Adamses the "tremendous burden" that their destiny was to lead the nation's foreign and domestic affairs. Raised with such expectations these men could hardly be satisfied with anything other than political success. Some of those who didn't achieve this success lived unhappily and died young.

You can try to understand how members of a family relate to one another. If possible, try to get concrete information about what actually happened within a family rather than relying only on nebulous impressions such as "Mother and Father loved each other very much" or "Jack and Susie were distant from each other." How did people show affection to each other? How did they show hostility? Did parents fight with one another? Did brothers and sisters fight? Was physical violence used in the disciplining of children or in conflicts between adults? How were disputes resolved? What kinds of alliances formed within the family?

Finally, you might want to ask whether life within your family has become more unstable in recent years. A major issue in today's public controversy over family life is whether or not the modern family is disintegrating. Although we now hear a few bold social critics proclaim the need for radical changes in the family, more familiar is the complaint that America's social ills are tied to an erosion of family stability.

Yet family historians have questioned whether this is really a contemporary phenomenon. Indeed, in the past, many Americans complained that the family was falling apart; some used the fear of family dissolution to resist social change. In the nineteenth century, for example, guardians of tradition warned that unless women devoted themselves to homemaking and remained pious, pure, and submissive, the family would collapse and society would fall back into barbarism. Versions of this same argument became a mainstay of the forces against women's suffrage.

Commenting recently on the family controversy, Tamara K. Hareven, an early student of family history, wrote that the specter of a declining family "has haunted American society" since the Pilgrims first settled on Plymouth Rock. "Every generation," she noted, "seems to be witnessing difficulties and to be predicting the family's collapse." (Do your older relatives recall feeling that the family was in danger earlier in this century?) Historical changes in the family, Hareven insisted, reflect the family's "diversity and flexibility," rather than its declining health and vitality.

Historians have suggested that rising divorce rates, although significant in themselves, do not necessarily mean that family life is more precarious now than in the past. Their work suggests that anyone exploring the thesis of the collapsing family (including the historian of one's own family) should consider many different factors. In America today, remarriage rates are high, which means that most divorced people resume life within a family group. Marriage opportunities are greater now than before, and although more families are disrupted voluntarily by divorce, fewer are disrupted involuntarily by death, disease, and economic distress. In colonial and nineteenth-century America, people were less likely to complete a full life cycle that included marriage, child-rearing, and middle and old age. Americans today have many fewer children, live to more advanced ages, and enjoy better health than in the past.

ATTITUDES AND BELIEFS OF FAMILY MEMBERS

We all make assumptions about the world that govern how we respond to experience. We may believe, for example, that people are basically generous or that they are greedy. We may be outraged by people who smoke and drink or by people who try to control the behavior of others. You can learn a great deal from exploring similarities and differences in the beliefs and attitudes of family members.

You might, for instance, want to enter the inner realm of family life that includes love, affection, romance, and domesticity. Following the lead of Philippe Ariès, some historians have argued that profound changes in how people regarded love and romance affected the isolationist instinct in families which accompanied the emergence of industrial society. According to Edward Shorter in *The Making of the Modern Family,* the dictates of custom gave way in the modern world to romantic love between spouses and bonds of sentiment between parents and children. Domestic life within the family came to be sheltered from the world outside. Children came to be valued for their own sake, and their welfare became the preeminent objective of parenthood. Personal happiness rather than "family interest" or economic advantage came to be the primary objective in selecting a husband or wife. Sex came to be appreciated for the emotional and physical satisfaction it brought, and not just for its part in procreation. Shorter's arguments are quite controversial among historians and should suggest to you many questions that you could ask about your own family history. How "modern" were the attitudes and beliefs of the members of your historical family?

Another area of interest that might not have occurred to you is family mythology. In his study of the Adams family, David Musto discussed the notion that families fashion myths that are passed on from one generation to the next. Musto contends that a family myth is a common view of the world and the family's place in it. The myth "is reinforced by family members" and becomes a "schema through which they interpret external events." What myths have existed in the families of your heritage? How has family mythology changed over time? For example, did family members believe that their destiny lay in tilling the soil, in sailing the seven seas, in serving a king or a country? Did family members identify the members of other families as their friends or foes (remember the Hatfields and the McCoys)? Did family members consider themselves to be descended from nobility? Did they believe themselves to be more upright, more intelligent, or more capable than those outside the family? Was there a family curse or a family prophecy?

Another matter to explore is people's attitudes toward their ethnic heritage. Despite the production of full libraries of work on ethnicity, the process by which people form and maintain an ethnic identity is still poorly understood. Most historians no longer believe that America is a great melting pot in which immigrants are fused into a common culture. But no generally accepted version of the assimilation experience has yet been articulated. How do people in your family define their ethnic identity? Are they simply Americans, or are they perhaps Afro-Americans, German Americans, or Jewish Americans? Do people retain emotional ties with nations other than the United States? Do they feel a special sense of comradeship with others of the same heritage? In a family that combines many ethnic groups, how do people decide which, if any, to identify with? Is there evidence in your family of an increased ethnic consciousness in recent years? If you can identify immigrant ancestors, you might want to explore their attitudes toward the country they left and the country they came to. How did an ancestor feel about the old country before immigration? How did he regard the old country after having spent some time in the United States? Which customs and beliefs of the home country did he retain? What aspects of American culture did he adopt? What attitudes, values, and beliefs did he pass on to his descendants?

Family stories may disclose something of what ancestors thought and felt. One girl attending the Smithsonian Institution's Festival of American Folklife told a revealing story about her immigrant ancestors. She began by noting that people are always puzzled about why she is both an Italian and a Presbyterian. To explain this oddity, she tells about her Uncle Alfred, who led the immigration of an entire Italian village to the United States. The immigrants were so anxious to become Americans that they decided to abandon their old ways of life, including their religion.

> And to them, being Catholic was very, very Italian and something to give up. To be an American was to be Protestant, and that's what they wanted more than anything. So when he came over, my uncle Alfred became a Presbyterian minister. And all the people who came over with him, about two hundred of them, became Presbyterians, too. And so today in Hamburg, Pennsylvania, there's a whole church of native Italian Presbyterians.

It is also productive to examine the rituals and routines of family life. If you are interested in religious beliefs and attitudes, you would want to learn how the family actually practiced their religion. Did the family hold prayer sessions? Did children say prayers at night? What prayers did individuals recite? Did someone say grace before meals? Did family members read the Bible out loud? Did people attend church? Were children confirmed or bar mitzvahed? Did the family keep any objects of religious significance? Did they perform any ceremonies involving these objects? If you intend to inquire about how people regarded their ethnic heritage, you might want to look at the food they ate and the practices they followed when preparing, serving, and eating a meal. In a study of "ethnic foodways," historian Alan Kraut has pointed out that food and rituals involving food are both "boundaries between members of different ethnic groups" and a means by which individuals can maintain an ethnic identity. In studying the foodways of a Jewish family, for instance, you would want to find out if they fasted on Yom Kippur, the day of atonement, if they ate the traditional Passover meal prescribed by religious law, and if they followed the Passover ritual of asking questions about the meaning and significance of the Passover ceremony. You would want to know if the family kept a kosher household, following such dietary laws as avoiding pork and shellfish, eating only animals slaughtered according to Jewish law, never mixing milk with meat, and maintaining separate utensils for meat and dairy meals.

The investigation of beliefs and attitudes could extend to any aspect of life. The following brief list of questions suggests some additional topics that you can investigate.

1. What special roles in family life did your ancestors assign to mothers, fathers, and children?
2. How did family members regard the elderly?
3. How did they consider the world of the child to be different from that of the adult?
4. What criteria did family members have for success?
5. What determined prestige within the family?
6. What did your ancestors consider to be immoral and moral behavior?
7. How did people regard the work they did? Their employers? Their fellow workers?
8. How did people regard their government? Their neighbors? Their church?
9. What did they think of such national leaders as Franklin Roosevelt or Huey Long?

10. What did they think of people prominent in their community?
11. What did they think of public policies such as trust-busting or the New Deal?
12. What aspects of their life did your ancestors believe to be within their control?
13. What aspects of life did they believe to be beyond their control?
14. What did family members believe their economic and social position to be?
15. Did they believe themselves to be the victims of exploitation or discrimination?

GEOGRAPHIC AND SOCIAL MOBILITY

America has long been a society of people on the move. Compared to other parts of the world, we are a nation of recent immigrants; all of our ancestors, except for those of Indian or native Hawaiian heritage, arrived here some time during the past four hundred and fifty years. During the colonial era, England supplied most of the European immigrants to what has now become the United States. But Spaniards settled in the South and the West, and Germans, Irish, Scotch, Scotch-Irish, Scandinavians, French, and Dutch settled in the Northeast. Until the ending of the slave trade in 1807, traders also brought approximately a half million black African slaves to North America. During the mid-1800's a new wave of immigration brought vast numbers of Irish, Germans, and Scandinavians to the United States. Many thousands of Chinese and Japanese also journeyed to America, but in 1882 the government officially closed the gates to Chinese immigration. During the last two decades of the 1900's, the tides of immigration shifted, and people arriving from southern and eastern Europe—Russians, Poles, Hungarians, Italians, Greeks—far outnumbered those arriving from northern and western Europe. This "new immigration" was slowed to a trickle by restrictive legislation of the 1920's, which was not substantially modified until the 1960's. In the years since World War II, Asians, Latin Americans, and Canadians have made up a much larger proportion of the immigrants arriving here than during any earlier period of American history.

Tracing your immigration history can be one of the most exciting of all family history projects. You might find that your ancestry includes only one or two nationalities (my own ancestors are from Russia and Poland) or that you are the result of a mixture of many ethnic groups (one student found that her family tree included people of Spanish, Italian, German, Scotch, and Irish descent). For each separate line of immigration you will want to learn where your ancestors came from, why they left, and how they traveled to America. Many English immigrants of the eighteenth century, for example, traded several years of labor as an indentured servant for passage to the New World. Many European immigrants of the late nineteenth and early twentieth century left from the German ports of Bremen and Hamburg. Some immigrants had walked to these port cities from far in the interior of Europe. What hardships did your ancestors face on the journey to the New World? Whom did they travel with? Did they have difficulty gaining entry to the United States? Did immigration officials change their surname? Whom did they meet in the United States? Did they settle with relatives or with friends from the old country? Did they stay in the port of arrival or journey onward? Did they live in neighborhoods dominated by members of their ethnic group? What did they bring with them from the old country? Did they ever return to their homeland? If so, why? What contacts did they maintain with the old country? How much money did they have? Could they speak English? What did they know about the United States? What employment opportunities were open to them? How were they treated by native Americans? By other immigrants? How did they regard members of other nationality groups? Did people refer to them with such ethnic slurs as "kike" or "wop"? Did they use such names when referring to others? Did they send for other members of their family? Did they help other immigrants arriving in the United States? Did they become citizens? When? Did they become part of a political organization, of a mutual aid society? Did they read newspapers of their nationality group?

Arrival in the New World did not mean that people ceased looking for new places in which to live. Immigrants to North America have continued to be a mobile people, fanning out across the continent and wresting vast quantities of land from the native Americans. In the seventeenth century, settlers from the Massachusetts Bay Colony (Boston) filtered into western Massachusetts, Connecticut, Rhode Island, and New Hampshire. Throughout the colonial period, people from the East crossed mountain barriers to settle in the wide strip of territory that reached to the Mississippi River. In the mid-nineteenth century, pioneers flocked to the mining frontiers of the Rocky Mountains and the territory farther west. Later settlers filled in the Great Plains that stretched between the Mississippi and the Rockies, the last stronghold of the American Indian. The official closing of the American frontier in 1890, however, did not signal the end of migration within the United States. Major streams of migration in the twentieth century have included the exodus of black people from the states of the Old Confederacy; the departure of farm dwellers for urban communities; the flight of city dwellers to the suburbs; the movement of Northerners to the Sunbelt of the South and Southwest. And in each year of our history, many Americans have moved to new locations, creating patterns of migration too complex to be recounted in any historical survey.

If you investigate the migration history of your ancestors you should consider not only where they moved but also why they moved, what they experienced in the process of moving, and how they fared in their new homes. You should become familiar with maps, perhaps even tracing the routes they followed. Try to compare the migration experiences of your ancestors with those described in works of history. Did your great-grandfather travel west in a covered wagon? How did his life compare to the stories told in textbook accounts of the movement westward? Did he experience severe hardship crossing the Great Plains or the Rocky Mountains? Did he carry a gun, join a vigilante group, or live in a Western boom town?

Social mobility generally refers to movement upward or downward in terms of social standing, prestige, income and wealth, education, or occupation. The opportunity for upward mobility has been a major part of the American dream of progress and success. According to this view of American life, America has always been an open and fluid society in which people could improve their own position in life and could expect continued advancement for their children. There have always been abundant opportunities for those who work hard and, since the mid-nineteenth century, a public school system that rewards talent irrespective of background. Neither the presidency nor the social register nor the board rooms of General Motors are beyond the reach of any American.

Some historians have begun to challenge this rosy version of the American Dream. They argue that by the eighteenth century American society had already divided into distinct economic classes and that movement from one class to another had become very difficult. They maintain that those who began life in rags could not expect to end life with riches no matter how frugal, hard-working, and virtuous they were. Instead, mobility has been a step-by-step process that doesn't always happen and often requires great sacrifice. Rather than advancing the most able students, the educational system has simply sustained the status quo by favoring the children of the middle and upper classes over those of the poor. Further, mobility for the great majority of Americans—blacks, Catholics, Jews, women—has been impeded by barriers of discrimination. These historians also claim that options open to people may have been limited by attitudes springing from within the family itself. The cultural heritage of some families, for instance, opposes the employment of women outside the home. The serious debate over social mobility in the American past is just beginning; the evidence is mixed and much more research remains to be done.

Generalizations about social mobility, of course, can't account for the experience of your own family. You will want to investigate the jobs people in your family held, the income they earned, the education they received, the wealth they accumulated, the offices and positions they held, the disabilities they suffered, the honors and accolades they garnered. You will want to look at what happened to people during their own lives as well as from one generation to the next. These two distinct facets of mobility are generally termed *intragenerational* and *intergenerational* mobility. In either case, downward as well as upward mobility can occur. My own grandparents, for instance, coming from Russia to America, never achieved the level of prestige or economic standing that their parents had attained in the old country. You should also be aware that advancement in one sphere of life doesn't necessarily mean advancement in all spheres. For example, in his classic study of social mobility in nineteenth-century Newburyport, Massachusetts, Stephan Thernstrom found that immigrant families were able to accumulate wealth and property only at the expense of education and possible occupational advancement for their children. These children often contributed their labor to the family, rather than striking out on their own.

THE FAMILY AND THE OUTSIDE WORLD

Be sure to consider interactions between your family and the outside world. You may not understand from your own experience how authority exercised by government and private interests affects people's personal lives, including such basics as love, companionship and respect, physical comfort and security. Alex Haley's work was inspiring partly because it showed how black people forged and sustained deep family relationships even though the slave master and the state threatened and often used their authority to disrupt the family.

Your own ancestors may have occupied a position in society very different from your own. They may not have viewed the police, the schools, the courts, their employers in the same way that you do today. And those with power and influence may not have looked upon your ancestors in the same way that they look upon you and your family. One girl of German descent whose family had lived in America for more than a hundred years first began to understand discrimination when she learned from family stories how her great-grandparents had been denied jobs and housing early in the twentieth century. She had never felt that her nationality restrained her freedom of action; in the past she had seen discrimination as something experienced only by other people.

In your own studies you might want to consider how both individuals and organized groups affected the lives of family members. Who was considered to be an outsider and not a family member? How did someone gain entry into the family? Did a nonrelative influence family members at turning points in their lives? Did family members form special bonds of friendship or enter into business arrangements with members of other families? How did people in the family relate to residents of their communities, to individuals who shared their religious beliefs or ethnic backgrounds? What was the nature of interactions between family members and those of different races, religions, and heritages? Were family members the victims or the perpetrators of discrimination (or perhaps both)?

Organizations like the church, the business firm, and the government may also influence family life. For example, a notable trend of the nineteenth and twentieth centuries has been that organizations outside the family have increasingly assumed responsibility for the family's welfare. Families have become more and more dependent upon the judgment of trained experts—social workers, physicians, psychologists, lawyers—and upon public institutions—hospitals, asylums, and old-age facilities. Especially in the post–New Deal era, families receive much more financial support from the government and pay far higher taxes than in the past. In looking at the interplay between families and outside organizations, you should keep in mind several broad issues. What functions did the organization perform? Did the organization have the authority to disrupt family life? Was this authority exercised? Did the organization pressure the family to adopt certain values? Did the organization restrict or expand the options open to family members? Whom did family members see as controlling the organization? What were their interests and objectives? What conflicts erupted between the family and the organization?

Do not, however, approach your family history locked into the assumption that outside intervention in family life is unique to our own time. In colonial New England, for example, there was little separation between the family, the church, and the government. Colonial magistrates could punish husbands or wives for using "ill words" and could break up poor families to relieve burdens on the public treasury. They could forbid persons of the opposite sex to meet with each other and could order the reconciliation of couples that had agreed to separate. Colonial officials could also place orphans, the children of "unseemly" parents, indigent individuals, and even criminals in the households of respected citizens.

Even in closely knit Puritan communities of the seventeenth and eighteenth centuries, however, the attempt to dictate the conduct of family life wasn't completely successful. With the breakdown of religious authority and an increasingly mixed population, the close ties between the state and family had weakened by the eighteenth century. Nonetheless, in New England and elsewhere, local governments continued to pass laws regulating family life, and people often felt it their duty to keep tabs on their neighbors and ensure conformity. Even on the raucous American frontier, attempts to maintain community control over family conduct often followed the founding of new settlements.

The major events that historians usually write about and which a family cannot control—wars, depressions, natural disasters, technological discoveries, and political movements—may have a profound impact on life within the family. In studying how such events affects the families of your ancestors, you will be moving into territory that historians are just beginning to explore. We still know very little about the effects of significant historical events on the personal experiences of individuals and families.

Glen Elder's study, *Children of the Great Depression,* is one of the few attempts to explore this question. Using information collected over several decades, Elder studied the effect of economic deprivation during the 1930's on a sample of families from Oakland, California. Elder found that not every family suffered severe economic losses during the period. Indeed, his work pivots on a comparison between those families that he terms "deprived" and those that he terms "nondeprived." Elder found that families had to adopt new strategies—such as assigning children more adultlike responsibilities—to deal with unemployment and loss of income. Deprived middle-class families suffered more acutely from a loss of status and prestige than did deprived working-class families. Contrary to his expectations, he discovered that economic distress actually strengthened people's commitment to traditional family values. Young men growing up in these deprived families were more achievement oriented and tended to formulate career plans and assume responsibility at an earlier age. For young women, however, economic loss seemed to reinforce an orientation toward home and family. One interesting result that Elder does not pursue is that by 1941 most families had returned to the same economic position, relative to other families, that they had occupied before the crash. Middle-class families of 1929 were also middle class in 1941; working-class families in 1929 were also working class in 1941. If generally confirmed, this finding would have profound implications for what it has meant to be middle or working class in America.

Critics of traditional history have argued that what goes on in the local community has had a more decisive effect on the lives of Americans than the national events that usually capture the historian's attention. They maintain that we will have a distorted view of American history until we painstakingly explore the history of individual communities.

As an historian of your own family, you can investigate local events without assuming the professional historian's burden of trying to determine how to put together the pieces of local studies to achieve reliable and coherent accounts of national history. Many different kinds of community events might command your attention: the drying-up of a well, the experience of an especially severe winter, the opening of a new road, the outbreak of disease, the appearance of the first automobile, the building of a factory, the arrival of new ethnic groups.

Finally, you might also want to consider how family life in your past was influenced by long-term trends that people at the time may not even have noticed. What has declining fertility and decreasing mortality meant for the families of your past? What changes in family life have been wrought by the increasing availability of life insurance and other means of achieving financial security? How have families reacted to varying forms of government intervention in the family? You will, of course, be hard-pressed to answer such difficult questions unless you possess information that covers several generations.

THE STUDY OF INDIVIDUALS

Another possible option is to focus on the lives of individual ancestors. You might attempt an analytic study in which you try to understand an ancestor's life and his or her world view, and how and why his or her life unfolded as it did. Many of the issues already discussed would be relevant to this type of inquiry. You might also be content with a more factually oriented account of a person's life. The following list includes some of the basic information about an individual that might be of interest to the family historian.

1. Name and place of birth
2. If deceased, date, place, and cause of death
3. Religious affiliation
4. Race
5. Nicknames and ethnic or religious names
6. Surnames and the reasons for their change
7. Marital history
8. Names of children and dates of their birth or adoption
9. Names of stepchildren; date of acquisition
10. If any children deceased, date, place, and cause of death
11. Occupational history
12. Military-service history
13. Political affiliations and activities
14. Offices held with dates

15. Medical history
16. Legal history
17. Income and wealth during lifetime
18. Land held during lifetime
19. Notable possessions
20. Languages spoken and read
21. Immigration history
22. Citizenship history
23. Skills and hobbies
24. Forms of recreation
25. Special achievements and accomplishments

In composing the history of an ancestor you may want to re-create the atmosphere of his times, delving into both national and local history. Draw on his memories of notable events and individuals, including those that may not have directly influenced his life. Did your grandfather ever see Bill Tilden play tennis, attend a performance by Enrico Caruso, or watch Babe Ruth belt a home run? Does he recall the Great Red Scare of 1919–1920? Did he believe that the Bolsheviks were about to take over the country? Did he ever hear a speech by Woodrow Wilson or listen to Roosevelt's first fireside chat? What did he do to celebrate the end of World War I and of World War II? For whom did he vote in the presidential election of 1932? Why?

If you want a family history full of flesh-and-blood characters, one that tells you how people felt about one another or how a depression affected family life, don't limit yourself to genealogical facts. Choose your own approach to the past, consciously planning a project that is meaningful and important to you (see Chapter 7), but be sure to ask the right questions at the beginning of your research.

In exploring family history through oral interviews, think about how to plan, conduct, and record sessions with your relatives. Oral history is a readily accessible resource, but it can be squandered by poor preparation, slipshod procedure, and unreliable records. A little attention to oral-history techniques will save you later frustration and vastly increase the yield of your research.

Chapter 3

HOW TO DO ORAL HISTORY: Conducting, Recording, and Interpreting Interviews

IN A TALK ON oral history interviewing delivered at the Oral History Association's First National Colloquium in Oral History, Charles Morrisey remarked that "to reduce interviewing to a set of techniques is, as one person put it, like reducing courtship to a formula." Morrisey added that while no set of rules can flawlessly guide the oral historian through every situation, anyone doing oral history should become familiar with methods of oral history that have proven successful in the past. Once you're familiar with the standard techniques, you may then want to devise procedures of your own.

CHOOSING YOUR INTERVIEWEES

It would be nice if details of family history could emerge unbidden at such family gatherings as picnics, Christmas reunions, or Sunday dinners, but actually one tends to find out very little of significance at such gatherings. People at family affairs want to catch up with each other and not dwell on a relative who has died years ago or feelings that are long forgotten. Relatives also tend to repeat the same stories over and over again. So if you are really serious about getting information you should plan even informal interviews in advance.

In compiling a list of prospective interviewees, cast your net widely at first and then worry about whom to actually contact. Be sure to consider interviewing aunts, uncles, and cousins as well as direct ancestors; within one or two generations, each of these relatives will have an ancestor in common with you. In addition to members of the family, consider talking to friends, acquaintances, employers, employees, co-workers, teachers, and business associates. Individuals from outside the family may offer a different slant on events and may be able to supply information unknown to relatives. If, for instance, your grandparents have died, are there any old friends still living who can tell you something about your grandparents' lives? You should also consider interviewing people of all ages, not limiting yourself to the elderly. By going up and down the family tree you can cover the greatest number of generations. Also remember to interview yourself or have someone else draw out your own knowledge and memories.

In deciding whom to interview first, take into account your emotional relationship with each informant. Although you might think that you should begin by interviewing your parents if they are alive, no relationship is more laden with emotion. For your initial interview choose the relative with whom you are most comfortable. This person might be a parent, but he or she is more likely to be a grandparent or even an uncle or aunt, since many of the emotional barriers between parent and child are not present between other kin. When you gain experience and proficiency as an oral historian, tackle the hard interviews with relatives who don't have much in common with you, who relate to you with difficulty, or who are likely to bristle at the idea of being interviewed. Not all people are easy to deal with, but the most prickly of relatives might be harboring the most revealing of stories. Don't discard potential subjects simply because you might expect them to be cranky or uncooperative.

In some cases you might not have the luxury of interviewing people at your convenience. If a family member lives far from home you might not want to travel to his residence simply to conduct an interview. Consider instead using a mail questionnaire with the prospect of conducting a personal interview on the occasion of a family visit.*

There may also be elderly people in your family whose memories you will want to record as soon as possible. So often, time runs out and precious memories are lost forever. My colleague in family history Joan Challinor laments that the "longest list in my life is the list of people I wish I had interviewed about family history before they died. The list is led by my Aunt Connie who was born in 1882, and must have slept with her eyes open since she never missed a single family event, happening, or detail." Aunt Connie died at the age of ninety-four, and most of her memories died with her:

> She was bedridden the latter part of her life, and I made it a point to visit her for some part of every day during the time we were together during the summer. We talked about everything: New York in the 1880's, New York in the 1890's, what it was like when there were only horse-drawn wagons

*See the Appendix for examples of questions that could be included in a written document. These questions are illustrative only. They are not designed to cover every topic or probe issues in depth. An actual questionnaire should be adapted to your own interests and family, and it should include ample space for responses.

> and gas lights, about Consuela Vanderbilt's marriage to the Duke of Marlborough, which was the grandest wedding New York had ever seen. These were the memories that I let slip by. I never taped a single talk. I thought I could remember her stories, but of course I can't.

When approaching an older person for an interview, never let on that you are afraid the elderly relative is about to die and that you must record his or her memories before it is too late. This attitude is reminiscent of that displayed by a relative who visits an elderly person in the hope of getting mentioned in the will. You want to convey instead that your subject has a valuable store of memories that you hope he or she will share with the whole family.

In pursuit of oral history you might find yourself tracking down relatives whom you have never met or even whose existence you hadn't suspected until they were mentioned by another family member or referred to in written material. If you know where such relatives are likely to be living, you might locate them by writing letters of inquiry to people with the same surname you find listed in the telephone book. (Of course, this technique works best if the name is unusual or the place very small.) You could also advertise in newspapers or in magazines such as *The Genealogical Helper* (P.O. Box 368, Logan, Utah 84321), which are designed to get individuals working on the same families in touch with one another.

APPROACHING YOUR SUBJECTS

Before deciding how to conduct an interview you must approach your prospective subject and gain his or her cooperation. This often takes a great deal of persuasion, because even the closest of relatives might be reluctant to participate in a family-history interview. If you meet resistance, be patient and considerate, but also be persistent. You may even ask other relatives or friends to intercede on your behalf. Professional interviewers often must go through a ritual of request and refusal before finally securing an interview. You may find that some relatives will put you through a version of this same ritual.

There are many reasons why people might be reluctant to talk about their past. A relative might feel that he is an ordinary person with no worthwhile history to contribute. He might imagine that he will be interrogated like a witness at a trial, or that he will be forced to divulge embarrassing information. You should explain to people that everyone has a story to tell (authors claim that we all have one great novel pent up within us), and that you are very interested in their memories. Indicate that you need their help to understand the family's history, and that you don't intend to pass judgment on their lives. Make it clear that you don't plan a third degree with rapid-fire questions and answers, but a respectful exchange between two people journeying into a past that concerns you both.

In every case lay your cards on the table right from the beginning. Using deception to gain an interview is as impractical as it is unethical. If you are not honest and open with family members you'll quickly find all your sources of information drying up. Clearly inform each interviewee what the purposes of your research are and precisely what you intend doing with their testimony. Make it clear that, at their request, you will keep confidential all or any part of what they tell you.

As an oral historian you assume a great deal of responsibility. You are asking family members to divulge in good faith intimate details of their personal lives and their relationships with other people. Your responsibility is to treat your informants with respect. If possible you should try to share your insights with those who have helped you, giving to family members as well as taking from them.

Before actually conducting an interview you might want to prepare family members by writing or telephoning them about what you plan to discuss. Advance notice can bring to mind events that they might not recall without time for reflection. Writing or calling ahead also indicates your interest in the project and demonstrates your respect for the person you are about to interview. On the other hand, you may not always choose to describe in detail what you plan to pursue in an interview, since this might kill a person's spontaneity or start him thinking about how to edit his memories.

Try to conduct an interview in the subject's home rather than in an office or in your home. People are usually most comfortable in their own home, the setting most closely associated with family memories. By taking the trouble to visit with someone, you show your interest in them and in the project. Also, a person being interviewed at home might unexpectedly produce pictures, heirlooms, and documents that supply fresh information. Try to hold your talk in the room in which the subject feels most at ease; often this will be the kitchen or the dining room rather than the formal living room. Choose a time for an interview when other demands on a person's attention and activities are likely to be at a minimum. Nothing is more disconcerting than trying to conduct an interview when someone is continually breaking off to make telephone calls or is anxiously awaiting the arrival of dinner guests.

TYPES OF INTERVIEWS

In planning oral history, take account of what you want to learn from the informant. Interviewing can be topical or autobiographical in approach. A topical interview is designed to obtain information about particular topics or themes that the family historian has isolated in advance of the interview—for example, in formation on the contents of a photograph album, family expressions and traditions, or such issues as privacy within the family, ethnic allegiances, religious practices, work, decision-making, or the impact of World War II or the Great Depression.

An autobiographic interview does not center around preselected topics, but tries to trace the flow of significant events in an individual's life. It need not be restricted to specific incidents such as moving to a new town or finding a job. It can include more general aspects of a person's life: his impressions of people, his political views, his ambitions and his defeats. You and your subject should together decide what to emphasize. You can also combine the two types of interviews, asking questions about particular topics before launching into a more general discussion.

A family historian must also decide whether to take a formal or an informal approach to each interview. In a formal interview, preset questions are asked in a rigid sequential order, with a minimum of probing or explanation. The formal interview achieves greater uniformity than a less-structured approach and enables a researcher to put together large numbers of responses and to report statistical results. But as a family historian you are probably more interested in obtaining the richest possible understanding of a person's life than in doing statistical analyses, so the informal interview is more appropriate.

Informal interviews range from entirely nondirected conversations in which the family member guides the discussions to interviews built around a flexible sequence of open-ended questions. Entirely nondirected interviews are appropriate when you want to learn what stands out in someone's own mind and how he understands and interprets his world. Rather than imposing your own priorities on the interview, you would let the subject decide what is worthy of discussion, complete with his biases and predispositions. Your questions would be few in number and designed to keep the interview moving rather than to direct what is being said. By letting the individual tell his own story, you get to know him more intimately. As folklorist and historian Richard M. Dorson says, "What the oral folk historian wishes to record is not the plain unvarnished fact but all the emotions, biases, and reactions aroused by the supposed fact, for in them lie the historical perspectives of the folk."

Nondirected interviews may also be appropriate when you have not yet focused your inquiry or when a family member is intimidated by a more structured format. For a first interview you might want to combine a few factual questions about people, places, and dates with a nondirected interview about the person's life. You might then follow up with a more formal session, taking either the topical or the autobiographical approach.

You should expect nondirected interviews to be highly anecdotal, full of stories about family experiences and personal opinions. In all interviews, be prepared to add, delete, modify, and change the sequence of questions. Follow up unexpected responses, and ask your relative to clarify or expand on his remarks.

THE SEQUENCE OF TOPICS

In planning an interview, use whatever you already know about a person's history. The more homework you do beforehand, the more productive the session is likely to be. You may know that Aunt Sylvia grew up on a farm, for example. Discuss that aspect of her life in the first interview. Once you've established an interview relationship with her, you can come back a second time to talk about her work with the Works Progress Administration during the Great Depression, or her feelings about her adopted son.

The sequence in which you broach various subjects can greatly affect what you learn from an interview. Initially you want to establish a good rapport with your informant, put the person at ease, interest him in the interview, and encourage him to talk openly and honestly. As in the example of Aunt Sylvia, start with matters that are likely to arouse a person's interest, that can be discussed easily, and that are not threatening or embarrassing. You might, for example, toss out some questions about a pleasant memory of childhood or about an accomplishment or triumph. You can phrase these early questions in a very general way that allows the person a great deal of latitude in deciding how to respond. Also, don't start an interview with a string of dull factual questions that will probably bore your informant and keep him from elaborating on his responses to more general questions. You may throw out a few factual questions at the beginning, but save the rest for late in the interview or even for a separate written questionnaire.

Always avoid shifting gears abruptly during an interview, and maintain some kind of logical progression of subject matter throughout. For example, don't begin a session with your uncle by asking about the death of his wife or about methods of family planning. Reserve such questions for later in the interview when you've established a good rapport. Introduce sensitive questions with tact and discretion and perhaps explain your reason for touching upon such matters. Don't spring threatening questions at the very end of an interview. By this time the person is probably getting tired and is likely to be annoyed and inclined to answer such questions quickly and superficially.

WORDING YOUR QUESTIONS

In addition to preparing topics and selecting their order of presentation, you should consider the actual phrasing of questions. In Gilbert and Sullivan's play, the Mikado of Japan is concerned to "let the punishment fit the crime." You should be equally sensitive to how your questions fit the purposes of your inquiry. Experts in survey research know that the wording of a question can decisively influence the response.

In a particular interview you might want to ask both closed and open-ended questions. A closed question usually gives the respondent a predetermined list of categories from which to choose his answer. An open-ended question allows the family member to answer a question any way that he sees fit. Closed questions are typically used when the possible answers to a question fall into a limited, well-defined range. They save time and allow you to compare the responses of different subjects; answers can also be recorded easily. Closed questions might relate to religious preference, number of languages spoken in a household, and number and type of people residing there. Closed questions may also be appropriate when you want to rank responses according to some quantitative distinction. For instance, you might ask a family member whether his recreation activities always, mostly, rarely, or never include members of his family. When using closed questions, make sure that your list of choices for each question exhausts all possible responses.

Most questions asked in most interviews should be open-ended. Open-ended questions don't include a list of possible responses; they may simply direct an informant's attention to a particular subject, allowing him broad latitude in deciding how to respond.

For example, you might ask a relative "What happened when you moved from the farm in Iowa to an apartment in New York City?" This broad question allows him to describe an incident, to report his feelings, and to discuss his own or other people's actions. But you might also ask a relative "Did the crowds of New York City make you feel uncomfortable when you arrived there from Iowa?" This much narrower question about the same situation asks the respondent to consider only his own feelings about a certain aspect of his new home. And it suggests that a yes or no answer would be sufficient. Broad questions tap the family member's own definition and interpretation of situations. They encourage the family member to give you a lengthy response, possibly including information that you hadn't anticipated. Narrower questions simply elicit specific information about some previously defined aspect of a situation.

You can phrase your questions to seek either an account of what happened or a revelation of people's attitudes and emotions. Be careful to distinguish between these types of questions and to choose the one that suits your purpose. Even more importantly, do not confuse a person's current opinions or sentiments with those of another time. You will often want to ask about people's thoughts, feelings, and experiences over a long period of time, bringing an interview right up to the present. The difference between how we once regarded people and events and how we now regard them can be striking and significant. Commenting on a childhood memoir that she had written, author and critic Mary McCarthy confessed that she had unwittingly misstated childhood feelings about her grandmother. She wrote that "in one sense, I have been unfair here to my grandmother: I show her, as it were, in retrospect, looking back at her and judging her as an adult. But as a child, I liked my grandmother, I thought her a tremendous figure. Many of her faults . . . were not apparent to me as faults."

Don't assume that you must always ask a direct question to get the information you want. The best approach to some topics might be to devise indirect questions from which you can deduce answers to your puzzle. People may be reluctant to talk about sensitive matters or unable to state the implicit ideas and attitudes that guide their behavior. Your grandmother, for example, would probably not know how to answer a point-blank question about the conventions of visiting and entertaining among her group of friends in her small town. But you might be able to answer this question yourself from how your grandmother responds to inquiries about when people visited one another, what kind of notice they gave, and what refreshments they expected to be offered.

The questions you ask a family member should be clear, brief, and simply phrased. Try to avoid questions with multiple parts or questions that the person you are interviewing can't be expected to understand. You wouldn't ask the same questions or use the same words for a college professor that you would for someone with a grade school education. Don't be patronizing, but don't shoot over your interviewees heads either.

Virtually every question you ask in an interview includes something that is assumed to be true. If, for example, you ask a relative about moving from Iowa to New York City, the question is based on the assumption that the move took place. If you ask him how often he visited the relatives remaining in Iowa, you assume that he made such visits. Assumptions are necessary for research; without them we would have to reconsider all that is already known every time we begin an inquiry. But when a question you ask incorporates an unreasonable assumption, the question may be said to beg another question. If you ask, "How did it feel to leave your family in Poland and journey to a hostile land?" you are assuming that an immigrant left his family behind in the old country and that he found the United States to be a "hostile land." Question-begging can, however, be much more subtle. Once common error is to word a question so that it implies either that things have definitely changed from past to present or that things have really remained the same. Always be sure to check for unwarranted assumptions that should actually be posed as questions.

In general, you should also avoid questions that reveal your own biases—such questions, for example, as "Uncle Arthur was an ornery old codger, wasn't he?" Likewise, the question "Didn't you feel oppressed to be working as a common laborer for twenty years?" suggests to the person that he really must have been oppressed and also debases the job that he held. Professional interviewers have developed techniques for effectively using questions that display a bias or influence the respondent. But until you become very experienced and proficient in the art of interviewing, you should probably steer clear of such questions.

You should be wary of loading questions with emotional words that may distract a relative from accurately recalling the past. When referring to an earlier time, avoid the use of words like "funny," "old-fashioned," "quaint," and "odd." People don't like having these adjectives applied to their early life and may unconsciously become hostile witnesses for the rest of the interview. Also be careful about biasing questions by referring to the past in language from the present. Reactions to the contemporary implications of these words may influence people's recollections of the past. If you were interested in feminism, for example, you might want to learn about your grandmother's experiences as a young woman of the 1920's. You could ask her about the women's movement of the time and the Equal Rights Amendment (the Woman's Party first proposed an equal rights amendment in 1921); about abortion, homosexuality, childbearing, and child-rearing; about relationships between boyfriend and girlfriend and husband and wife. But you would be well advised to phrase your questions in ordinary language and not load them with contemporary political terms such as "women's liberation," "right to life," and "gay power."

PROPS AND OUTSIDE INFORMATION

The mainstays of many an interview may be the "props" that you bring along with you, including documents and material objects. You might want a relative to identify and relate the history of a letter, a family heirloom, or an old photograph—both to cross-check facts and to gain different perspectives on events. Props are a means of jogging memories, of getting relatives to recall people and events long forgotten or to enrich their recollections with additional detail. A person you are interviewing may look at an old watch and exclaim, "Why, this belonged to Uncle Marvin! They gave it to him when he retired. What an awful time the family had finally persuading him to stop working. I remember . . ." You might not have gained half as much insight merely by asking the relative to tell you about Uncle Marvin.

Responses to props may be quite different from what you expect. Our family has a splendid picture of my grandmother in her wedding dress, taken in 1917. It's the kind of picture that you would use to show people how beautiful your grandmother really was. But when my sister showed our grandmother this picture, she responded by saying how awful she had looked during the wedding and how the dress wasn't what she had wanted. She complained that they simply couldn't afford a really nice wedding.

To obtain independent views of the past you might want to use the information contained in other sources without actually showing the source to your informant. You might, for instance, have a letter from your grandfather's brother describing what happened when your grandfather ran away from home as a teenager. You may choose to ask your grandfather about this incident rather than actually showing him the letter or relating its content. Otherwise you might find that your grandfather is reacting to what is in the letter and to his feelings about his brother rather than giving you his own recollections of the incident.

THE INTERVIEW SESSION

No matter how carefully planned, a poorly conducted interview will be frustrating for both you and your subject. You may learn less than anticipated or be misled by the results of the interview. The family member may finish the interview feeling exploited, belittled, or even insulted.

Good interviewing is a difficult art that develops slowly with experience. Don't expect your first few efforts to be masterpieces of oral history.

For a successful interview, you must resist the inclination to argue with relatives, to correct their memories, or to pass judgment on their lives. You must be able to remember what you've already asked, to determine how well a person is answering the latest question, and to anticipate what you'll ask next. You should know how to probe for additional information without interrupting the flow of memories. You should be able to shift subjects smoothly and to take advantage of new developments while guarding against excessive digression.

The best interviews are usually conducted one on one, without other people present in the room. Interviews with more than one person are obviously necessary when a relative doesn't agree to see you alone, when you feel a relative would open up more easily with another present, or when you specifically want to foster discussion among family members. Generally, however, another person's presence will inhibit a family member, especially on sensitive matters. You will find it difficult to interview several people at once, and you may be unable to follow their responses.

LISTENING

Every family historian must listen much more carefully than one does in ordinary conversation. Most of us rarely experience the pleasure of having someone listen attentively to what we say. Good listening establishes rapport with a subject and encourages open communication. Elderly people especially may feel they have been "put on the shelf," ignored by younger generations. Your showing a real interest in the memories of an elderly person in your family may come like rain on parched ground. If your interview did nothing more than show one older person that he or she still has much to give, something that others cherish, your interview would be a success.

Careful listening is essential if you want to learn from an interview rather than simply confirm what you already think you know. In their classic work *Methods of Social Study,* Sidney and Beatrice Webb warned that "The first, indispensable factor in successful investigation or fruitful observation . . . is an efficient attention. . . . Indeed, most people without being aware of it would much rather retain their own conclusions than learn anything contrary to them. . . . To be a good listener, you need to hear what others have to say."

Careful listening includes attention to the volume, tone, or inflection of a remark and to such nonverbal clues as gestures, facial expressions, eye movements, and changes in body position. Raymond L. Gorden of Antioch College has observed that even those who "have learned to hide certain nonverbal clues to their feelings and attitudes" cannot exercise complete control. According to Professor Gorden, a person "might display a calm facial expression and a casual tone of voice, yet betray anxiety by twisting his hands." As you gain experience in oral history you will learn to watch a person's total response to the questions you ask.

Make a concentrated effort to understand (although not necessarily adopt) a family member's point of view. To be a good oral historian you need an open mind that lets you take in what a person is saying without automatically dismissing what seems unreasonable or recasting testimony to fit your preconceptions. During the interview try to listen to events from the other person's perspective. This may never be entirely possible, but we can make more of an attempt at it than we normally do. My own grandfather, for example, fled service in the anti-Semitic armies of the Russian czar only to face being drafted into the U.S. Army during World War I. Fifty years before the Vietnam War, he left the United States for Canada, to escape fighting in a war that he considered profoundly unjust (like Vietnam, many Americans opposed our involvement in World War I). To his dying day my grandfather still believed that the government would try to prosecute him as a draft resister from World War I. I *knew*, of course, that my grandfather was perfectly safe. But if I had simply dismissed his fears as the paranoia of an old man, I would have missed learning a great deal about his personality and about how he viewed the United States and its government. Fear of prosecution, I found out, was so real for my grandfather that he never became a naturalized citizen and wouldn't let his wife become a citizen either.

Don't assume that if you tape-record an interview, you can simply listen to the tape at your leisure, catching anything that you may have missed at the time. You may never find the time to listen carefully to all your tapes, and before you can return to a tape, impressions of an interview will probably already be set in your mind. Careful listening during an interview also helps you avoid embarrassing gaffes like asking about the health of a relative whom your grandmother just told you was deceased. Most importantly, close attention to an informant is necessary to ask follow-up questions, to return to unanswered questions, to ask for clarification of or some elaboration on one or another statement, to adapt to unexpected information, and to recognize contradictions and inconsistencies. An oral historian who is not a good listener will be paralyzed by his prepared set of questions and unable to benefit from what turns up during the interview itself. A good family-history interview will take on a life of its own, following paths that may be very different from those you had originally planned to travel. You may not get answers to half your questions, but you may also get twice as much family history as you expected.

PROBING FOR INFORMATION

Unless you are ready to exploit the unexpected you may lose fascinating details of family history. During the course of an interview a relative might refer to an incident that you hadn't known about, reveal an unsuspected side of an ancestor's personality, or contradict your understanding of events. In response to an innocuous question about her children, for example, an immigrant grandmother might remark that she had an abortion before giving birth to her first child (many immigrant women of the early twentieth century did in fact have illegal abortions to avoid having children they couldn't afford). Unless you followed this revelation up with tactful yet penetrating questions, you might never be able to learn why she had the abortion, where she went, how she felt, or how her husband reacted (if he knew about the abortion at all). By forfeiting your immediate opportunity and planning to return to the matter during a later interview you may lose this significant episode of family history. You may never conduct the next interview or your grandmother may never again be willing to talk about the abortion.

Be prepared to ask for clarification and elaboration. Thomas Mann once replied, on being accused of making his books too long, that "what is not detailed is not interesting." It is this detail that you must seek by judiciously probing for more information. A relative of Irish descent, for instance, might mention that he grew up in an ethnically mixed neighborhood of New York City. Rather than letting this casual remark pass by, you could ask him what the neighborhood was like or question him specifically about what ethnic groups lived in the neighborhood and how they related to one another.

Don't be satisfied during an interview with vaguely phrased responses. Try to get a family member to translate such responses into concrete ideas and actual behavior that can be checked against information from other sources. For example, your grandmother might tell you that she came from a large family. Ask her how many brothers and sisters she had. Your grandmother might go on to say that her father was a brilliant man. But what does she mean by "brilliant"? What achievements of your great-grandfather led her to this conclusion? Did he have advanced degrees, speak many languages, or work at an intellectually demanding job? Did he speak or write beautifully, or show great wisdom in resolving family disputes? Often legends of people's brilliance (or dullness) develop in a family without much foundation. Mary McCarthy wrote of her own father that "as for the legend that he was a brilliant man, with marked literary gifts, alas, I once saw his diary. It was a record of heights and weights, temperatures and enemas, interspersed with slightly sententious 'thoughts,' like a schoolboy's."

Try, if possible, to find out a person's sources of information. A great-uncle might describe what happened the first time your late grandparents met. But was he an eyewitness to the meeting or only the recipient of a later account? Was he in a position to observe what happened, or was he so involved in his own activities as to be an unreliable witness?

Sometimes you have to follow up an initial question because a family member responds with "I don't remember." Your worst reaction in this situation would be to challenge the family member by insisting that surely he or she must remember what happened. You should instead allow the person time to think; perhaps indicate that you can appreciate his or her difficulty. If you still get no results, try using whatever you already know to stimulate the person's memory. You may, for instance, be asking your grandfather about the time he ran away from home, an incident mentioned in a letter written by his brother. If your grandfather can't remember running away even after being given some details from the letter, show him the document itself. If he still can't recall the incident, you should entertain the hypothesis that for some reason your great-uncle actually fabricated the story.

Even if you do not immediately probe a family member's response to a question you can return to the question later in the interview. Indeed, a good way to test the accuracy of a story is to reserve probing until other topics have been discussed.

As an interviewer you might find it illuminating to ask about contradictory information revealed at different times during an interview. In response to a question at the beginning of an interview, your grandmother might tell you that her father was an unsociable man who treated the family with cold formality. Later, however, she might mention that her father sometimes brought her little gifts and even called her by a pet name. By asking tactfully about this apparent inconsistency, you might learn that your grandmother was her father's favorite and that she would occasionally see his warm and tender side. To take full advantage of an interview you should try to keep track of whatever is said; don't think that once a question has been answered to your satisfaction you can afford to forget about the answer.

There are a great many reasons for probing what a relative tells you during an interview. The following list summarizes the kind of information you might seek through follow-up questions.

1. The proper sequence of events
2. The exact role played in events by each individual involved
3. The continuation of a story
4. Examples of general statements
5. Definitions and explanations of vague terms
6. Further details in a description
7. The reasons for holding an attitude, sentiment, or opinion
8. The reasons for changes in attitudes, beliefs, and opinions

9. Contradictions or inconsistencies in what a person says
10. Contradictions between what a person says and what other sources suggest
11. How an informant came to know what he says he knows

INTERVIEWING TACTICS

Be sure to probe a family member's responses with care and tact. Don't try to show off your skill at repartee or display the range of your knowledge. Avoid pressing so hard that you offend or confuse your informant. Be thorough in your questioning, but don't rapid-fire questions. Memories are not likely to flow freely in an atmosphere electric with tension. A family member who feels that he is being interrogated is likely to respond with shallow and evasive answers, thus defeating the purpose of your interview.

Try to avoid arguing with respondents or contradicting what they tell you. Under some circumstances argumentative or even bullying questions may prod a person to expand his descriptions and fully explain his ideas. But this approach may also outrage your informant. If, for instance, an aunt says that your grandfather was a stern, authoritarian parent, you may want to test the strength of her convictions by tactfully pointing out that "Uncle Irving believed him to be a very indulgent father." (Of course, you aren't trying to "correct" her memories of your grandfather; you simply want to have them clarified and expanded.) You may, however, decide to use a less challenging means of gaining further information (and one that's easier on Uncle Irving). Use your own good judgment and your knowledge of family members.*

*Some textbooks on interviewing recommend that you not identify the source of contrary information. But this may not work well for family-history interviews, since a relative is likely to inquire about your source.

Don't let your probing entwine you in small matters of fact that can be ascertained some other way. If an elderly relative tells you she graduated from high school in 1917 and you stop her to maintain that it was really 1916, that may end the discussion about school. She may have been planning to tell you that she really wanted to go on to college, but that her father wouldn't let her because he didn't approve of higher education for women. Her reasons for failing to attend college and her father's views on education for women are much more important for understanding family history than the actual date of her graduation. In that case you've lost far more than you've gained. If necessary, dates and nitty-gritty facts can always be fitted in later, either by questioning or the examining documents.

Digression should be tolerated for a while, since interesting and unexpected insights may emerge. A good rule of interviewing is to avoid interrupting your informants unless they clearly are digressing to no useful purpose. Remember too that interruptions can be nonverbal—a startled look, a raised eyebrow, or an intake of breath while a relative is relating an embarrassing episode can quickly deter any further revelations.

People should be given time to answer questions and to think about their answers. You should not jump in because you are nervous about silence. When you ask a question, wait. After a person seems to have completed an answer, give him some extra seconds. Look to see if he seems to have finished his comment or is still thinking about your question. Don't be afraid of pauses that may last twenty or even thirty seconds (which may seem like an eternity to you). Americans seem to be constitutionally averse to silence. But properly timed and spaced pauses create a deliberate and thoughtful mood during an interview, contributing to depth of response. You will find that attempts to fill quiet spaces with nervous chatter or hasty questions will generally be counterproductive.

Of course, too much silence can be uncomfortable and embarrassing for both interviewer and subject. It can drain the life out of an interview and suggest to an informant that you aren't doing your job. Be deliberate, but not agonizingly slow. Try to respond as best you can to the family member's own pace and expectations. And you can accompany silences with nonverbal expressions of interest and alertness.

FAMILY TRAGEDY AND SCANDAL

There may come a time when a perfectly neutral question brings up some truly unhappy memories. A picture of a young man, unknown to you, may turn out to be the portrait of a beloved cousin who died in a war or went west to seek his fortune and was never heard from again. You will have to show that you empathize with your informant. If you are made uncomfortable by tragedy and even tears, you will have to learn to tolerate them if you are to be a good interviewer.

During an interview session you also may unexpectedly uncover a family scandal. Don't think that family scandals are simply amusing stories about the family's black sheep or the horse thief from the nineteenth century. (My own family has a black sheep, Uncle Morris, who was last seen peddling cheap goods on the sidewalk at 42nd Street in Manhattan, fleeing the approach of a policeman.) Family scandals can remain acutely embarrassing or deeply disturbing to relatives today. Depending upon the values of family members, a scandal can involve an illegitimate birth, an interracial marriage, a murder within the family, a marital infidelity, a financial swindle, a draft evasion. Listen attentively to the events described, and don't interrupt the account with expressions of outrage, shock, or dismay. Be ready to probe cautiously for elaboration or clarification of the story being told to you. And of course you must respect the family member's right to preserve the confidentiality of his testimony.

No fixed rules govern the confidentiality of oral testimony. Each family historian must work out individual agreements with each of his informants. A family member may give you permission to use his testimony as you see fit, or he may ask you to maintain the confidentiality of all or some of his remarks. He may also ask you not to quote him directly on certain matters, while giving you license to summarize his comments. When dealing with especially sensitive testimony you should consider fashioning a written agreement between yourself and the person you interview. For an introduction to the legal issues raised by the practice or oral history, see the 1973 issue of *Oral History Review.*

ENDING AN INTERVIEW

Concentrated interviewing is tiring, especially for older people, so bring the interview to a close after about an hour or an hour and a half. After that point you may be getting poor-quality responses to questions that could be asked another time. However, be flexible. If a relative is pouring out fascinating information beyond the hour and a half, let the interview continue. In some cases, you may want to take a break and return again to the interview, particularly if you could not easily arrange another session. After an interview be sure to thank the person and let him or her know how much you enjoyed the session. If possible stay and chat for a while. This shows your interest in the person and contributes to a good feeling about the interview. You might also want to use this time to ask about any other sources of family history that the relative might possess. If people feel that they have supplied worthwhile information and don't feel drained or exploited, there is no reason why you couldn't come back another time. Before you leave, try to arrange the next interview. Or if you plan no further sessions, indicate that the person should get in touch with you if he or she comes up with additional information.

RECORDING AN INTERVIEW

Should one take notes or not, tape-record the interview or not, transcribe the recordings or not? These questions must be faced by every oral historian. The problem is how to get as much as you can out of an interview without spending great sums of money or sacrificing vast amounts of time.

TAKING NOTES

The answer to the first question is a simple one: *do* take notes. Note-taking is an essential part of the interview process that shouldn't be abandoned without very good reason. During the interview your notes are an instant reminder of what your informant has said, alerting you to matters that should be embellished. Without notes you would have to retain this information in your head or sacrifice opportunities to ask follow-up questions. Don't try to record every word said, or seem so buried in your papers that the subject feels ignored. Instead, jot down key words and phrases and try to paraphrase major points. You may even want to write down quickly the follow-up questions that occur to you while listening to the interviewee. These interview notes can be very rough, relying heavily on abbreviations, incomplete sentences, and personal codes.

Later, you can use these notes to write a permanent account of the interview. Do so while the session is still fresh in your mind. If possible, include both the questions you have asked and the responses supplied by the family member. Abbreviations, incomplete sentences, and code words in your notes should be translated into ordinary language. In your written account you can expand your notes with your memories from the interview and add any nonverbal cues that you have picked up. You might relate your general impression of how well the interview succeeded and summarize your most important findings. After finishing your write-up, take some time to plan your next meeting with the family member.

TAPE-RECORDING

Obviously the greatest accuracy in preserving a person's memories is achieved when you supplement your notes with a tape recording of the session. Although the tape recorder is a useful addition to the note pad, the whir of spinning tape should never substitute for the scratching of a pen. A tape recording will neither help you follow a relative's reminiscences during the interview nor record his gestures and expressions. You may not find the time to listen carefully to the tape and write down the crucial information it contains. But reference to a tape can expand your notes, clarify points that seem confusing, and help with names, dates, and places. The tape may reveal aspects of a person's responses that you missed, or correct your misconceptions. It also preserves your own questions, which may be difficult to keep track of while conducting an interview. You can return again and again to a tape, listening to remarks that may not have seemed important at the time but that take on great significance in the light of information from other sources. Moreover, a person's voice is a valuable record in itself that brings you closer to the individual and his memories.

On the other hand, using a tape recorder may have serious drawbacks. Recording can be expensive; you need to buy, rent, or borrow a recorder and purchase tape for each interview. Family members can be intimidated by the notion of being taped or even freeze in front of the microphone. Another reason for not abandoning notes is that although the tape recorder is a simple mechanical device, many mechanical things can go wrong. I've had tapes break and batteries go dead in the middle of an interview, and I've run out of tape and missed the last few minutes of valuable testimony.

Be sure to gain permission from the person you are interviewing before tape-recording a session. If a family member flatly refuses to be taped, you must accept his wishes. If a person is willing but apprehensive, you may allay his fears by chatting informally while the tape recorder is running and then playing back this bit of conversation. People who haven't been taped before are often surprised to hear how their own voice sounds, and this can help break the ice and get an interview going (this is also a good opportunity to make sure your equipment is functioning properly). Eventually the interviewee will forget about the recorder unless you keep fussing with it.

Be thoroughly familiar with your equipment before you conduct an interview. Practice beforehand until you become sufficiently profficient to operate your recorder automatically, without having to stop and think about what to do next. If you are collecting tapes for your own use, you probably should use a cassette recorder with a built-in microphone that can be placed between you and your subject (be sure to clean and de-magnetize the recorder heads regularly). Cassette tapes generally vary in length from one to two hours, half on one side and half on the other. Ninety-minute tapes are a good choice for most interviews. Shorter tapes must be turned over more often, with greater risk of losing information. Longer tapes are more likely to break, jam, or lose the quality of their sound. If possible, plug your recorder into a wall socket rather than relying on batteries, and bring more tape than you think you can possibly use. (If you plan to do a lot of interviewing, try buying your tape in bulk.) If you don't have a warning signal at the end of a tape, be sure to turn the tape before a side runs out. Don't worry about leaving a minute or two of unplayed tape at the end; just flip the cassette and start recording on the other side without rewinding. If you are unsure about the quality of the sound you are getting, from time to time play back a second or two of tape. Do this as naturally as possible, without interrupting the flow of the interview.

Take good care of your tapes once you have taken the trouble and expense to record an interview. Tapes should be clearly labeled (your name, the name of your subject, the date of the interview, and the place where it was conducted), placed in their containers, and stored in a clean, dry place, preferably with a constant temperature of about 70 degrees and a humidity of about 50 percent. Rewind your tapes at least once a year to maintain proper tension and resiliency and to avoid having sound "leak" from one strand to another. By all means keep your tapes away from magnetic fields—such as, for example, an electric motor—that can lead to their erasure. Take the time to create a separate index of each tape. Your index can divide a tape into five-minute time segments, and indicate the major points covered in each segment. It can also list the people mentioned on each portion of the tape. This indexing can save you much time and anguish later on. It's enormously frustrating to listen to a ninety-minute tape searching for mention of Uncle George when Uncle George appears only once at the end of another tape.

Generally you will not want to transcribe your tapes verbatim. Transcription requires special playback equipment and an excellent typist with a fine ear for the spoken word. Even a proficient transcriber using the best equipment will take several hours to type a single hour of tape. You will then have to comb through the transcription for accuracy, typographical errors, and proper spelling, punctuation, and grammar. This, too, can take several hours. Willa K. Baum, director of the Regional Oral History Office at the University of California, estimates that it takes "an average of six to twelve typing hours for each hour of recording."

INTERPRETING ORAL HISTORY

Oral history is evidence consisting of other people's memories from which you try to piece together an accurate picture of the past. Although a person's recollections may seem to speak for themselves, you must use your knowledge and reason to draw conclusions from what you are told. If, for example, your grandmother tells you she was born in Sweden in 1898 you would probably assume that this was true without even stopping to think about it, since you expect people to know where and when they were born.

Yet your conclusions about your grandmother's birth are not necessarily facts but inferences about an event that you didn't observe. Indeed, those with experience in family history know that people are often unreliable reporters of their own birthdays. Immigrants in particular may have reconstructed their birth dates from guesswork or may even have lied to get married or qualify for a job. By the time a person is seventy or eighty years old, the reality and the distortion may have become inseparable.

You can learn a great deal from oral history, but without adequate precautions you can easily jump to misleading conclusions. You should approach oral evidence with open-minded skepticism, eager to learn but suspicious of even what seems most obvious. As Sherlock Holmes once remarked, "There is nothing more deceptive than an obvious fact." Always ask yourself the question "Why has the person I interviewed related this testimony to me?" You may find that there are several plausible answers to this question, for people's accounts of the past are several steps removed from what actually happened. Human beings aren't faultless recording machines. When a relative describes an incident he has experienced, we know that his initial impressions of the event are likely to be incomplete and shaped by his own biases and expectations. But the family historian's problem doesn't end here, for in addition to the fact that our memories are notoriously fallible and selective, what we recall seeing often changes as our own ideas and attitudes change.

Like the testimony delivered in a court of law, the oral history recounted by your informants deserves the most careful study. What a family member relates during an interview should neither be cavalierly dismissed nor uncritically embraced. The following questions should assist your evaluation.

What do you know about the general credibility of your witness? Some people are mortified to tell a lie (perhaps afraid their nose will begin to grow); others delight in making up tall tales and deceiving members of the family. Some folks are inclined to exaggerate their achievements and overlook their failures; others are unwilling to admit they played a part in any event. Some people delight in ridiculing and disparaging their fellows; others wouldn't dream of uttering a word of criticism. Some folks are unwilling to confess even a small spark of emotion; others, like Lewis Carroll's Mock Turtle, weep and wail at the slightest provocation.

Does the witness have any biases or special interests? Bias and prejudice are usually resistant to change; rather than modifying our ideas in accord with new information, we may adjust what we observe and remember to conform to what we think and feel. A family member who always hated Jews, for example, would not be a reliable witness about anything concerning the first Jew to marry into the family. People may deliberately or unwittingly shade the truth to advance their personal interests. Would a family member benefit from having you believe a certain version of an incident in family life? Or might he be seeking to protect another member of the family? Keep in mind that interests need not be sordid or selfish. A relative may want the family to have the best possible impression of his mother and may thus exaggerate her virtues and understate her faults.

Was the witness in a position to observe accurately the events that he describes? All else being equal, people who see things firsthand are better witnesses than those who had to rely on others for their information. The original source may have lied, unconsciously distorted the truth, or been honestly mistaken. Accounts of events may also change by design or inadvertence as they pass from person to person. Family stories are often embellished with additional detail or exaggerated to increase their drama and excitement. An uneventful migration to California in the 1870's may be enlivened with skirmishes against Indians and fierce blizzards in the Rocky Mountains. Middle-class ancestors in the old country may be transformed over time into high nobility. Several different stories might be telescoped into one, or the basic structure of a story may remain intact while its time, its place, and even its characters are altered in the retelling. Often the person who originally told the story becomes its protagonist rather than its narrator. Anyone who has played the game of Telephone knows how a simple message changes after being told to five or six people. Think about what might happen to family stories transmitted across generations. In his renowned book *Oral Tradition,* Jan Vansina wrote that "initial testimony . . . undergoes alterations and distortions at the hands of all the other informants in the chain of transmission, down to and including the very last one, all of them being influenced by . . . their private interests and the interests of the society they belong to, the cultural values of that society, and their own individual personalities." You do not, of course, discard testimony that has passed through more than a single informant, but you treat it with special caution, and try to learn what you can about the original source and the process of transmission.

Even an eyewitness, however, may not be in a good

position to report the details of an event. He may have been too far away, too distracted, or too involved in the event to see and hear things accurately. You would be rightly skeptical of a participant's account of a family argument or one by someone listening several rooms away. A witness may also be unable to understand what he observed. Attorneys recognize that certain technical matters are beyond the competence of most people and require the testimony of qualified experts. Similarly, historians are wary of reports that go beyond the knowledge that could reasonably be expected of a witness. As a family historian you should, for example, be suspicious of a family member's version of what caused the illness or death of an ancestor.

How was the family member influenced by the interview process itself? People being interviewed know that they are producing a record of their own history that may be passed on to future generations. For most of your relatives this probably will be a new experience, different from the ordinary conversation of daily life. Some may strive especially hard to be as accurate and as candid as possible; others may be inclined to exercise more self-censorship than would be likely in a less formal setting. The testimony that you get in an interview will also be affected by the questions that you ask. You need to become introspective after an oral-history session, considering how your own questions influenced the responses of your informant.

In addition to asking these questions, you should carefully examine a person's oral testimony as a whole. Try to collate the records of every interview conducted with a person, looking for connections among scattered recollections. In response to one question, for instance, your grandmother might tell you that while she was in her early twenties she became active in charitable work with orphans. In answer to an entirely different question, perhaps even in another interview, she might tell you that her first child died in infancy without ever coming home from the hospital. Did the death of her child precede her commitment to working with orphans? Were the two events causally connected? Look also for contradictions or inconsistencies in a person's testimony and for accounts that seem implausible or clash with what you think you already know. The discovery of a contradiction or a seemingly false account should lead to further inquiry, but not to the automatic discarding of testimony.

As a family historian you can learn a great deal from what appears to be a contradiction in oral evidence. A graduate student exploring his family history uncovered fascinating information about his great-grandfather by trying to explain conflicts in his family's oral tradition. Family members reported that his grandfather said, "Although my brothers and sisters all lived a long life, I knew only one of them, my baby sister." Yet these same relatives insisted that his grandfather was a devoted family man. Why would such a pillar of the family not know his own brothers and sisters? The student finally solved the puzzle when he found out that his grandfather was the product of his great-grandfather's second marriage. After bringing this knowledge to the attention of other family members, the student found that someone remembered that the grandfather had never met the children of his father's first marriage. Eventually he learned the full story. His great-grandfather, it seems, was quite a lady's man; his flirtations with other women had eventually driven his first wife to take the children and flee. Undaunted, the student's great-grandfather charmed another woman into marriage and began a second family that included his grandfather, the family man.

When analyzing testimony, try not to oversimplify what a person has said by forcing complex experience into categories that are easy to understand and seem to present a clear picture of what happened. Try to catch the subtlety, the ambiguity, the nonrationality of actual experience. Interviewing specialist Lewis Anthony Dexter recalled that he has been the subject of several interviews about his political activities. Almost invariably, he reported, the interviewers "tried to make the story I reported to them more coherent, more 'rational' than in fact it was." He noted that "the interviewers wanted answers reporting sharply motivated behavior, whereas in fact, so far as I could recollect, we acted in response to a complex and often inchoate set of desires and beliefs which could not be stated sharply." Dexter's remarks should serve as a warning against an overly schematic approach to oral history.

The testimony of relatives is neither inherently reliable nor unreliable. Rather, the reliability of evidence must be judged in relation to the questions being asked. Often testimony that can't reliably answer questions about external events can disclose much about people's values, attitudes, and expectations. Among the stories told by visitors to the Festival of American Folklife are two tales about the Civil War. One person told about her great-great-grandfather who was a "non-veteran" of the Civil War. His mother, it seems, paid for a substitute soldier, a commonly used and legal means of avoiding military service. On Memorial Day, her ancestor's family would stay at home, hiding their shame behind closed shutters and locked doors. Another visitor told of an ancestor reputed to have been a wounded war hero, even to have walked with a limp for the rest of his life. Partly as a result of this story a military tradition had developed in the family. Recently, however, family members had begun to explore their history and had found that according to official records their ancestor hadn't fought in the Civil War at all; his family had likewise paid for a substitute soldier. Although this second family story may not accurately report what happened, it is good evidence for understanding the values of both the bogus soldier and the relatives who told and perpetuated the tale.

Questions about oral testimony can be answered by seeking independent sources of information. If you want to double-check a person's birth date, you could use oral reports from a sibling; dates on the backs of old photographs; a family Bible; or a birth certificate. Independent evidence of an episode narrated by a relative would include the accounts of other witnesses; letters, diaries, and journals; and even a newspaper story if the incident received public attention.

The marshaling of multiple sources is a powerful technique for reliably reconstructing the past. You can be more confident of a factual conclusion after finding distinct but corroborating bits of evidence. However, take care that additional sources do not merely repeat misinformation. If you want to double-check the birth date of your immigrant grandmother, an American birth certificate or marriage license would probably be based on the same faulty information you originally received from her. But agreement between your grandmother's report and a birth certificate from the old country or the testimony of an older sister would be more convincing.

Remember that relatives may have heard a story from a source several persons removed from the original event. If your grandmother told the same story to your mother and your aunt, a comparison of the sisters' accounts would only disclose how each of them changed the original account. Try to find the relatives whose first encounter with the story came from the source closest to the event.

When you find contradictions in the messages of different sources, don't simply try to decide which source is likely to be more reliable and discard the other as useless. Instead, find out why your sources conflict. If, for instance, a birth certificate found among your grandfather's papers lists his birthday as three years earlier than he had reported, you might be tempted to conclude that the official document is surely correct and that your grandfather's testimony should be disregarded. But if you again visited your grandfather and asked him about the discrepancy, he might tell you that the birth certificate was a forgery that enabled him to qualify for service in World War I. This revelation might lead to a new line of questions about your grandfather's history and bring to light aspects of his past that you might otherwise have missed.

When struggling to extract the most accurate conclusions from historical evidence, try to be sensitive to your own biases. Professional historians take care to give due weight to conclusions they find disheartening or offensive. Not everything in a person's family background is pleasant or uplifting. After studying the history of his family, psychiatrist Murray Bowen discovered along with people of achievement "a few alcoholics and a few who didn't do well." Dr. Bowen also confessed that "I found one murderer. That's the humanity of your family." As a family historian rather than a family censor, your responsibility is to confront the humanity of your family as honestly as possible without trying to reshape the past according to a vision of how things ought to have been.

The more ambitious family historian will integrate oral history with scrutiny of other sources. The more independent information you can muster, the more accurate and complete your reconstruction of the past will be. Different sources tend to capture different sides of family history. Marshall McLuhan's notion that "the medium is the message" can be applied to family history. A family photograph, for instance, might be excellent evidence for what people looked like, the kinds of clothes they wore, and the houses in which they lived. But photographs portray people's lives at frozen moments of the past and usually show the serene and pleasant side of life. Family stories, in contrast, emphasize action and change over time, often highlighting times of conflict and stress. Official records like birth and marriage certificates and land records might not be as richly detailed as oral testimony, but they may disclose information about names, dates, and places that surviving ancestors can't supply.

Research into one source may also guide the study of other evidence. An incident mentioned in a letter, a snapshot showing a family on vacation, or an inventory of wealth in a probate record may suggest many questions to be asked in an oral interview. And a relative may guide you to family documents or official records by telling you where an ancestor once lived, by recalling a distant cousin, by remembering an old trunk stored in an attic. The most productive and exciting projects in family history exploit a variety of source material, all of which are described in the following chapters.

Chapter 4

HOME SOURCES

NOT ALL RESEARCH that goes beyond oral history need take you to an archive or a library. Right at home you possess evidence invaluable to a family-history project. Your family archive includes letters, diaries, family Bibles, bills, financial ledgers, appointment calendars, birth certificates, licenses, and insurance policies. It also includes furniture, tools, jewelry, books, samplers, and quilts. Even a home and its environment or a place where an ancestor worked or is buried can be used as evidence for family history. The list on pages 86 and 87 indicates many of the home sources that you can study.

Home sources, of course, aren't likely to be neatly filed, catalogued, and ready for your inspection. You should not assume that people take the time to organize their papers and possessions or that they appreciate the value of items rich in family history. To locate home sources, be prepared to ransack attics, cellars, closets, trunks, and boxes for items long stored and often forgotten. Look in the pigeonholes of desks, pry behind the backs of photographs, and even explore the drawers in kitchens and bedrooms. One of my grandmother's kitchen drawers, just below the silverware, was crammed with papers and other items acquired over several decades.

Some of the most interesting documents and objects may be in the homes of relatives. If possible, enlist their active assistance in the search for home sources and alert them to the importance of preserving items that yield knowledge of the family's past. Don't be surprised, however, if relatives are reluctant to sanction a canvass of their personal papers. A family dispute or a youthful indiscretion might be hidden in dust-gathering documents that relatives would prefer to leave undisturbed. Family members may even be inclined to destroy or censor papers that you want to examine. Tact and diplomacy as well as patience in explaining the importance of accurate family history may go a long way in solving these frustrating problems.

HOME SOURCES

Family Documents	*Material Objects*
The family Bible	Books and magazines
Letters	Toys and games
Telegrams	Athletic equipment
Post cards	Records
Diaries	Tape recordings
Journals	Guns
Appointment calendars	Knives
Ledgers	Souvenirs
Account books	Maps
Bills	Ornaments
Canceled checks	Trophies
Bankbooks	Medals
Bank statements	Posters
Credit cards	Buttons
Employment records	Jewelry

Tax records
Social security card
Identification cards
Driver's licenses
Hunting and fishing licenses
Wills
Deeds
Bills of sale
Insurance policies
Stocks and bonds
School records
School assignments
Military records
Medical records
Prescriptions
Church records
Citizenship papers
Passports
Marriage licenses
Birth certificates
Baptismal certificates
Confirmation certificates
Court records
Yearbooks
Scrapbooks
Clippings
Awards and citations
Calling cards
Greeting cards and invitations
Recipe files
Baby books
Family histories and genealogies
Memoirs
Poetry
Clocks and watches
Coins and stamps
Bottles and cans
Boxes and containers
Bottle tops
Instruments
Appliances
Machinery
Locks
Metalwork
Tools
Furniture
Clothing
Needlework
Quilts
China
Silverware
Plates
Mugs
Glassware
Bowls and pitchers
Mirrors
Knick-knacks
Candlesticks
Rugs
Painting
Sculpture
Plaques
Religous objects
Photographs
Albums
Home movies
Houses and apartments
Factories, offices, and stores
Cemeteries

Be sure to keep an inventory of all items that you look at both in your own home and the homes of relatives. If you identify each document and object by a brief description or a code number, you can take notes without worrying about later having to match them with the appropriate item. You may also want to photograph home sources, particularly those in the possession of others. Although photographic reproduction is often accurate and striking, the camera may still distort perspective, size, shape, and distance or alter impressions of color, tint, and shading. You should be careful to take photographs from different angles and to supplement photography with written descriptions and perhaps even sketches.

Before using home sources to reconstruct the past, you must first judge the authenticity of documents and material objects. Is the evidence really what it appears to be? Occasionally a family historian may encounter a forged document, concocted perhaps to qualify for a job or to conceal a blemish in the family's past. To decide whether a document is genuine or forged, you need to examine the item with care and ask the proper questions. Are there contradictions in the information recorded on the document? Does this information agree with what you know from other sources? Does the document have the same form as similar items from the same time and place? Is it written on paper from that period? How did the document come into your possession? What was its previous history? Was anyone in a position to forge the document? Would anyone have benefited from a forgery? The analysis of documents, however, often poses complex technical problems. If in doubt, seek the assistance of qualified experts at a university, museum, or historical society.

Beyond outright forgery, you may confront more subtle problems of authenticity. Family heirlooms, for instance, may be difficult to identify or date. Even when heirlooms carry stories about who owned them, how old they are, who made them, and what they were used for, you should try to verify these accounts. Look for supporting evidence from family documents or take an heirloom to a museum or historical society. Also look for clues about dates and identity on the objects themselves. Samplers, quilts, and coverlets often have the name of the creator and perhaps even the date embroidered in the corner. Wedding rings, watches, silverware, and other objects may have engravings with dates of the special event and the initials of the recipients. Family jewelry and silver may sometimes have engraved monograms as well. Some objects may supply the name of the manufacturer and the place of origin. Others might be identified and dated approximately by looking at advertisements in newspapers, city directories, and magazines or by consulting the Sears and Montgomery Ward catalogues. Remember, too, that objects that seem strange to you today may once have been part of a household economy now supplanted by new technology. The mechanization of the household, which we all take for granted today, was a slow process that only accelerated after the turn of the century with the dissemination of the vacuum cleaner, the gas range, the electric fan, and other devices.

But the proper identification and dating of items might not solve all of your problems. Family members may have purchased perfectly legitimate antiques that were later passed off as heirlooms owned by the family for generations. So beware of the sampler on Grandmother's kitchen wall which seems to refer to your ancestry, for in fact Grandmother may have purchased it at a sale simply because the family name was on it.

FAMILY DOCUMENTS

For genealogists, the family Bible is the most important source in the home. Family members often record births, deaths, marriages, and baptisms in their Bible. Many Bibles have special sections for noting such information, but look also at the inside of the front and back covers and at the blank pages that may be inserted at the end of the text. A family might have one Bible replete with information that is passed from one generation to the next, often through the eldest son. If you can't find such a Bible, but suspect that one might exist, check through family wills, as the passing of the Bible was serious business in many homes. Another common tradition, particularly in the nineteenth century, was the presentation of a Bible to newlyweds. Not only would these Bibles eventually contain information about the young couple's family, but often items from the parents' family Bible would be copied into the new Bible. Do not assume then, that information in a family Bible was always recorded at the time that the events occurred. Mistakes could have been made in the transcription, or a family member may have reconstructed events from memory or guesswork. See if entries in a Bible are written in different colored inks or in different hands. Check the publication date of the Bible to see if any of the information predates the existence of the book.

For learning the details of your ancestors' experience and penetrating the emotions of family life, **letters** are possibly the most useful of all family documents. Although strewn with comments about the weather and other fillers of everyday writing, letters do offer revelations found in few other sources. Beyond vital information about births, deaths, marriages, separations, graduations, and the like, letters may include stories about vacations, accounts of political events, descriptions of courtships, and narratives of day-to-day life. They may express people's feelings and opinions and give their impressions of friends and family members. Letters may also refer to changes in the community, new acquisitions, or the condition of a family farm or business. David Brandenburg, one of my colleagues at The American University, has a set of letters from his great-uncle Alfred describing life as an American flier in World War I. Each of these fascinating documents came in duplicate. The letters Alfred wrote for his mother discounted the perils he faced and screened out the harsh side of combat. The letters he wrote for his father candidly reported his own situation as well as his honest impressions of the war. Great-uncle Alfred was shot down by the Red Baron's outfit one day after the Red Baron himself was killed. New letters then arrived depicting life in a German prisoner-of-war camp.

Consider the style and form as well as the content of family letters. You might find that your great-uncle Harry, whom relatives described as cold and forbidding, wrote warm and intimate prose to his wife and children. Reading his letters, you might revise your opinion of him. Relationships among family members can also be disclosed through the salutations and closings of correspondence. A person's style and vocabulary might reveal something about his education, his aspirations, and his values. In cards sent on special occasions, my grandparents would address their grandchildren as "dear and beloved" and close with "your loving and affectionate grandparents." Sometimes they would even sign their full names: Sam and Rose Lichtman. These cards were written not in ordinary prose but in flowery and sentimental poetry composed by my grandfather. Even the envelopes of letters give you details of family history. Postmarks and addresses may tell you where a family member lived or spent his vacation in a particular year.

Rarer than letters, but closely related in content, are **diaries and journals.** Especially for women, who often lacked other outlets for their thoughts and feelings, the diary was an important means of self-expression. Bound by leather or tied together by a string, diaries may supply details of both large events, such as marriages or funerals, and daily routine. More than any other source, a regularly kept diary offers a sense of the pace and rhythm of family life. Some diaries are little more than calendars, merely listing the day's events. Others discuss the writer's feelings about other family members, marriage, sex, money matters, and children. Because diaries are usually meant to be private, they may disclose thoughts and feelings that a person wouldn't dare express in a letter.

Often diaries will be found with clippings of old newspaper announcements, programs from dances, plays, and sporting events, photographs, **yearbooks,** and other mementos of a person's life. Or such items could be found in **scrapbooks.** You should ask yourself why a person considered such memorabilia important enough to save. Was a high school basketball career so important to your father that he saved all of his reminders of those days? Was every trip to a city so exhilarating to a farm-girl great-grandmother that she saved little souvenirs from each trip?

Before drawing any conclusions from a document you must first determine what your witness actually meant. You might encounter technical terms and jargon or even documents written in a foreign language. Also keep in mind that forms of handwriting change over time, as do the meanings of words and phrases. Assume that you found an early-eighteenth-century diary in which your ancestor refers to elderly people as "gaffers" or "fogys." You might spend considerable time wondering why your ancestor so disliked older people and perhaps even venture some guesses about his character from this information. Yet all your conjectures could be based on a misreading of your ancestor's written testimony. In a study of attitudes toward growing old, David H. Fischer argues that for most of the colonial period words like "gaffer" and "fogy" didn't have the same pejorative connotation that they have today. He suggests that as attitudes toward old age changed late in the eighteenth century, terms that once were neutral or even honorific changed in meaning to become terms reviling the elderly. Although you may not have any documents from colonial

America, you should be aware that words can change their meaning in a very short time. And you should be especially careful of how you read anything written by an immigrant ancestor from another culture.

Keep in mind that someone's motive for writing down his ideas and experiences will affect both how completely and how accurately he relates what he saw, thought, and felt. People noting episodes of family life in the Bible knows that they are writing for future generations and generally will try to be as accurate as possible. But those producing a record for posterity might also try to conceal what they find shameful: for example, the birth of an illegitimate child. Diaries are often considered windows into people's inner lives, because they supposedly are private documents written only for the author. But don't assume uncritically that a family diarist was blithely unconcerned about those who might someday read his or her entries. The Roman statesman Cicero wrote all his private papers with an eye to their eventual dissemination; he even instructed a slave to arrange them for posthumous publication. On the other hand, letters are often written for specific purposes having nothing to do with leaving an accurate record for historians. A letter written to a family member about the annual reunion, urging him to attend the next gathering, is likely to emphasize what was pleasant and exciting about the meeting and to contain no mention of what was dull and disagreeable.

In addition to consciously writing about their lives in letters, journals, and Bibles, people produce many kinds of records in the course of their daily lives. The family of the great critic H. L. Mencken saved virtually every scrap of paper connected with family life. From a carefully preserved bill we know that a doctor, one C. L. Buddenbohm, not a midwife, attended Mencken's birth in 1880. Not every family is quite this compulsive, but every family has some surviving records. Many people write wills to arrange their affairs after death. The final version of a person's will often can be obtained from probate records, but that person might have drafted several earlier versions which can be found among his personal papers. New revelations might emerge from following the evolution of a final will and conjuring explanations for the changes you observe. Financial transactions intersect many things that a person does. Bills, account books, ledgers, stocks and bonds, canceled checks, tax records, and bank statements may provide hints about the family's general financial condition and about business ventures. **Financial records** can also tell you where people went, what they bought, what services they used, what charities they supported, what clubs they belonged to, what politicians they favored. **Medical records** and bills give you an idea of family health and of how the family viewed both sickness and health. **Recipes** may offer insight into family culture and ethnic allegiances (and perhaps improve your own cuisine).

Families also save **official documents** from which information can be extracted. Military induction and discharge papers can lead you to other government records for additional information. Hunting and fishing licenses can tell a researcher something about a person's recreational activities. Passports can document someone's foreign travel, and church records his religious beliefs and activities. Various kinds of certificates may record milestones in an ancestor's life. Diplomas offer evidence about education, particularly about whether a person attended parochial or public school and what the minimum level of education he or she attained is. Naturalization papers have an almost religious significance for some families, as they officially announce that the family is American. They may be framed and proudly displayed on walls.

In combing through family papers you might come across a "big find" so notable that it changes the direction of your research. Some family historians have unearthed diaries from colonial America or the records of a business founded by an ancestor. Going through my grandfather's papers after his death, we discovered several hardbacked notebooks containing the minutes he had taken as secretary of a senior citizens' club. His records, written sometimes in English and sometimes in Yiddish, were detailed and meticulous and were written in a beautiful, flowing hand. They reveal much about my own ancestor, about the culture of Jewish immigrants in New York City, and about the special concerns of elderly people.

MATERIAL OBJECTS

Material objects, including items found around the home, a home itself, or a local cemetery, are more difficult to use than are written documents. Nevertheless, when thoughtfully approached, many seemingly commonplace objects can add to your knowledge of family history. Items like quilts and samplers may actually record such events as births and marriages. More than just supplying information, the things people owned and used also remind us of skills, habits, and styles of life that have now disappeared. A set of surveyor's tools or a roll-top desk might evoke the life of an ancestor, lending us a little of his physical presence that otherwise may seem so remote. When shown to a relative, objects often trigger a flood of reminiscences about an earlier time. If you locate your great-uncle's tools and place them before him, he will probably respond with stories from his working days. If you show your grandfather the chalice that he brought with him from Russia, he may better recall his life in the old country.

Try to find out as much about the history of family possessions as you possibly can. You should learn the oral tradition associated with an object and consult family documents, if possible, cross-checking information from these two sources. Objects that the family owns might have been mentioned in letters or referred to in wills and inventories. Precious items may have notes either attached to them or filed elsewhere.

By asking a few simple questions, you can begin learning about family history from objects found in the home. When did the family acquire the object? Why did they acquire it? How much did it cost? What was it used for? How commonplace was it? What was its quality? Was it handcrafted or mass-produced?

Also, try to find out why certain objects were saved and others discarded. In our consumer-oriented, mobile, and throwaway society, people find it expensive and cumbersome to keep items. Each move that a family makes usually reduces its store of papers and objects. The attic of one friend's aunt contains a neglected piano. When asked about its origins, the aunt replied that her father had won it in a lottery, and excited over actually winning something, he made his children learn to play the piano despite their protests. After his death, no one could stand the sight of the piano, but at the same time no one would take the responsibility for throwing it away. So the piano inhabits a corner of the aunt's attic, awaiting a Beethoven for its liberation. Not all objects have a story behind them, but attics, basements, and closets are filled with objects stored for sentimental or other reasons, and often they can reveal much about the people who owned and used them.

When beginning a tour of family possessions you will probably notice especially valuable and striking antiques first. These items may shed light on a family's financial position, its social status, its pride and aspirations. Items made by family members may reveal skill and craftsmanship. Objects specially selected by certain members of the family may reveal their taste and style. Monogrammed silverware and family portraits suggest both money and family pride; carefully preserved pewter spoons may not be suggestive of wealth, but may also bespeak family pride. A heavy oak desk or bed, constructed without a single nail, may display the skills of an ancestor. A Tiffany lamp purchased in 1912 might indicate a desire and ability to keep pace with the avant-garde.

To better understand found objects, dip into the voluminous literature on antiquities. A good place to start is the *American Heritage* series on antiques. Works are available on virtually every item that a family could conceivably possess. Usually these books are very expensive, so try your local library. The art index will lead you to specialized articles on any object of interest. Almost every object present in the home also has a club or society dedicated to its study and preservation. Plates, pottery, buttons, mirrors, and even bathtubs have inspired aficionados to band together in organizations. A reference librarian will help you get in touch with one of these clubs.

In your search for the significant and unusual, don't overlook more mundane, yet fascinating objects often found around the home. Tools, for instance, may tell you something about people's occupations. An old, black, heavily taped drill may have been used by your uncle during his mining days. Battered toolboxes may disclose the skills and devices of a carpenter at the turn of the century. Remember that such tradesmen as plumbers, masons, and bricklayers quite often bought their own tools and saved them after retirement. You may want to talk to family members and experts to see how the tools of a trade have changed over time. Does the change mean a lessening of skills, a decline in the quality of workmanship, or changes in the nature of a job? You may also check with a union local to find out if they know of any old-timers who remember how work was in a certain trade fifty or more years ago.

Religious objects can also be very revealing. Many tokens and symbols seem so ordinary that they are overlooked. Yet the distinctive design of a family cross or a menorah may give an indication of where your family came from or what particular sect they belonged to. A medal imprinted with the image of Saint Vladimir, for instance, suggests that your family may have come from Russia, for he is patron saint of the Russian Orthodox church, particularly of the Moscow patriarch. Unfamiliar objects may mean that religious practices have changed over time. If you are uncertain about the meaning or use of an item, check with local religious leaders; they may know the answer or be able to refer you to someone who does. Don't assume that your ancestors celebrated Christmas or other religious holidays in the same manner that you do.

Study of the objects used in recreation and sports may be critical to developing a well-rounded portrait of your ancestors' lives. Your predecessors didn't live only for work. Too often family histories have people striving to make a living or raise a family without touching on moments of play and relaxation. You might find a beautifully carved chess set that belonged to your grandfather, or your grandmother's mah-jong set, with the tiles all smooth and worn. (Do you know when mah-jong first became popular in the United States?) That strange round object in the closet might be a bocce ball brought over from Italy, or those peculiar-looking wooden sticks in the attic might be your grandfather's golf clubs. Remember that such seemingly standard pieces of sporting equipment as the golf club, the baseball glove, and the hockey stick have changed quite radically in appearance and construction over the past few decades. A taped broom handle may be a stickball bat used to smash drives over three manhole covers in New York City. A rusting gun may have been toted on hunting trips through woods that have since disappeared. Bring an old catcher's mitt to an uncle and you might learn how it felt to play semi-pro ball in the days before catchers wore masks.

There are those who say that we know people best from what they read. Study your ancestor's book collections, but be careful to distinguish between the books that he owned and those the family may have acquired later. What is the balance between fiction and nonfiction? What genres (for example, mysteries, adventure books, classics) and subjects (for example, carpentry, history, or sports) are included in the collection? Are any of the books written in languages other than English? (My grandfather's collection included works in English, Russian, and Yiddish.) Are there any books that seem not to have been read? Are there inscriptions on the flyleafs or marginal notes on the pages?

Other items that your ancestors collected can also reveal much about their interests and experiences. Did a family member amass travel souvenirs or collect such objects as stamps, coins, pistols, knives, dolls, china, or mugs? Did an ancestor seem to bounce from one interest to another, or did he or she become captivated by a hobby and stick with it until death? Have the hobbies and interests of family members changed over time? Can you gauge the influence of such new forms of entertainment as movies and television?

In addition to studying the objects that you find in a home, think for a moment about what you fail to find. A failure to come across items that you suspect an ancestor may have owned could mean that the items were lost, sold, given away, or discarded. Or it could mean that the ancestor never possessed the items in the first place and that your evaluation of him may have to be revised. If, for example, you find no religious objects among an extensive collection of your grandparents' possessions, you might find that they had renounced all religious affiliations as youthful radicals of the early 1900's.

Homes and other buildings, including offices and factories, are also records to be read and interpreted. To the casual observer, a building stands mute, unworthy of attention; to the family historian, however, a building is a home for a family, a place of work, or a business. Each structure has its own personality acquired over a period of time.

There are many questions that you can ask when looking at a family home or apartment. When was it constructed? What materials and methods were used? What style of architecture was followed? How many rooms does it have? How large are the rooms? What functions did they serve? What land does the home include? What kind of furniture does it have? What alterations and additions have been made over time?

Consider what people have learned from looking at the one-room farmhouses still standing on the eastern shore of Maryland. These houses may seem to be uninhabitable from today's perspective, but families of freed slaves once lived in them with pride. If you looked inside an old freedman's dwelling you would realize that a one-room structure is not simply a one-room home. Inside, the house was once divided into rooms without walls. The pegs near the entrance probably held coats and clothes to dry; the bench near the wood stove was probably the living room, where the family would gather to keep warm and talk. The shelves on the other side of the stove, with a table long gone, probably constituted the kitchen. Another corner, with a piece of a mirror, was likely the washing area. The bed probably rested in the last of the corners. Instead of relying on lumber, nails, and tiles, those who built the house used products found in the area—logs and pegs. Nearby, there might stand another house that belonged to the family just before people moved north in the early twentieth century. This house might be built with commercial lumber and building products, but inside it might be very much the same, except that walls now divided up the living space and additions afforded separate bedrooms to members of the family.

Be sure to record your observations of dwelling places, preferably by taking photographs and writing notes. Supplement these observations with the oral reports of family members or senior residents of a community.

This same method of observation and interview can be used in viewing an old factory or a mom and pop store.

All of the places where goods and services are produced, bought, sold, and transported have stories to tell. They can tell us about the conditions under which people worked, the kinds of tools and machinery they used, the routines they followed, the skills they possessed, the items they produced, and the services they offered. You can use maps, city directories, and tax reports to locate old buildings. Visit the area to see if the structures are still standing, and check to see if a former employee or son of an employee or a family member still remembers where the building stood. A walk through an old building might yield a lot of information. The family historian who prowls through an old cotton mill, for instance, might learn the amount of space allotted the workers, the positions in which they labored, the tasks they had to perform. He might even be able to imagine the noise and smells of the place, its lighting and ventilation. When looking at a factory or office, search for clues about dates, examine any machinery or furnishings, and look for unusual decorations. Remember, of course, that buildings change profoundly over time; a structure erected in 1898 may have had ten or more uses to date.

From the places where ancestors lived and worked, the family historian must turn to the places where they are buried. Inscribed on gravestones and monuments are names, dates of birth and death, and statements of relationships. These inscriptions might also describe notable events in the community or the special achievements of individuals. Cemeteries are cultural institutions designed to educate and inspire the living as well as inter the dead. The size and shape of headstones and monuments, the use of tombs and sarcophagi, the images engraved in stone, even the choice of a certain cemetery—all reflect ancestor's religious beliefs, their philosophies, and their ideas about what confers status and prestige.

THE CONSERVATION OF DOCUMENTS AND OBJECTS

Every family historian should try to conserve precious documents and objects. This does not mean that you should attempt to restore your possessions. Conservation is the attempt to maintain items in their current state of preservation, whereas restoration is the effort to improve their condition. Restoration usually requires the skill of an expert, but everyone should try to preserve and protect what he or she owns. Even if an item passed along in the family still seems to be in mint condition, do not assume that it will last without care. Paper can become faded and brittle, metal can corrode, clothing and wood can be attacked by rodents and insects. With proper attention, however, your precious heirlooms can be an enduring legacy to the family.

If you have an especially valuable item or face a difficult problem of conservation, seek expert assistance through local historical societies and museums. Most qualified conservators in the United States belong to the International and American Institute for the Conservation of Historic and Artistic Works. To learn how to conserve your heirlooms, you also can consult the vast body of specialized literature on conservation. In *Manual for Museums,* Ralph H. Lewis provides a good bibliography at the end of his chapter on caring for museum collections.

You can, however, become familiar with a few basic guidelines for conservation. Check all storage places for fire hazards, possible water leaks, and excessive vibrations. Try to maintain moderate and stable temperature and humidity. A temperature between 60 and 70 degrees Fahrenheit and a humidity between 40 and 60 percent is appropriate for most items. Keep strong light off your possessions, and try to protect them from dust, dirt, and pollution. Watch for signs of insects and other pests; if necessary, call on the services of a professional exterminator. Don't pile up fragile documents or stuff them in drawers. Don't put Scotch tape on items; mount them on ordinary paper or wood, lean them against one another, or clean them with common household products. In some cases, you may even want to purchase transparencies for covering documents, or acquire cabinets, shelving, racks, boxes, and containers specially designed for specific types of items. If you don't use such storage facilities, make sure to properly line drawers, shelves, and boxes. If you must transport items, pack them with great care. Always remember, when unsure of what to do, seek the aid of qualified experts.

Chapter 5

FAMILY PHOTOGRAPHS

Joan R. Challinor

THE PHOTOGRAPH AS HISTORICAL EVIDENCE

"A picture," the old saying goes, "is worth a thousand words." Yet genealogists and historians alike have devoted millions of words to the interpretation of written documents while scarcely pausing to consider what can be learned from family photographs and home movies. Almost every family has a gold mine of history in its collections of photographs. People who want to dig for their roots would do well to look also at the top of the tree—in their attic among boxes of family photographs.

Only during the last few years have historians turned to photographs as source material for studying the history of immigration, women, and the family. The historian who examines photographs as well as material objects, letters, and diaries can enter people's homes and glimpse details of their lives. The camera gives the historian another eye —not an eye with perfect vision, but one that can see what historians have not been able to see before.

Journalists and other observers of the contemporary scene have long used photographs to portray America and its people. During the 1930s, for instance, the Farm Security Administration dispatched such first-rate photographers as Dorothea Lange and Walker Evans to document the Great Depression, thereby lending an immediate reality to this experience for Americans who never saw the dust bowl or an apple seller. *Life* magazine brought photojournalism to new heights by presenting current affairs with great visual impact to millions of Americans each week. But journalistic photography captured families caught up in large political events and didn't convey much about everyday family life.

Your first task is to gather all the photographs and home movies your family owns. You can borrow photographs from relatives, have them copied, and return the originals. You don't have to copy every picture they own, but do select the most interesting ones. Be prepared to be shocked by the enormous number you will find. Immigrants newly arrived in America often managed to scrape together enough money to have themselves photographed years before they were able to own their own cameras. One historian whose ancestors arrived penniless in New York in 1889 found an unmarked box filled with well-preserved pictures from his grandparents' earliest days. His experience is not unique. No matter when your family arrived or in what financial condition, be alert for early photographs.

Each photograph that you find should be regarded as an original document of family history with potentially valuable information to impart. Obviously, photographs can tell you what your ancestors looked like at various times in their lives. You may be surprised to find your own features appearing in the photographs of an earlier generation. In *The Camera of My Family,* Catherine Hanf Noren wrote that "As the images emerged in the developer, I saw signs of myself: throughout my mother's family, for instance, the same hands, again and again, and they are my hands. My great-aunt Else, whom I had not only never met but never consciously heard of, was in physiognomy a sister to me. When I first saw her image I was stunned." But photographs can reveal details of family history even when you can't identify each individual portrayed. You can still find out how people dressed, what kind of furniture they owned, the kinds of houses in which they lived, the rituals they followed, the places they visited.

If your family has photographs that might pre-date the twentieth century, you need some basic knowledge about the history of photography. Photographic technique has passed through several stages of development since photography began in the 1830's. Any family historian can easily learn to identify the major types of early photographs. You do not need to become a chemist or a photographic historian to figure out what type of photograph you are looking at and to determine when that kind of photograph was popular. This knowledge can then serve as a guide in determining the date when the photograph was taken and can thereby help you to identify the subject. An ancestor who died in 1837 cannot appear in any photograph since photography first began in 1839. A relative who died in 1894 can't appear in a rectangular Kodak picture because until 1896 all Kodak photos were circular in shape. What follows is a brief tour of some popular kinds of early photographs.*

TYPES OF PHOTOGRAPHS

Photography began in 1839 when L. J. M. Daguerre, a Frenchman, discovered a method for preserving on metal the image that a box with a pinhole could throw upon a

*The discussion of nineteenth-century photographs relies heavily on the informative book by William Welling, *Collectors' Guide to Nineteenth-Century Photographs* (New York: Collier, 1976).

ground glass. To create a daguerreotype (1839–1856), the term for these earliest of photographs, a person sometimes had to pose for as long as twenty minutes. Later, as the technique was perfected, exposure time decreased but still remained very long by today's standards. To make sure that the subject would hold a pose for the required length of time most daguerreotypists in the early days seated the person before the camera and firmly clamped the subject's head in an iron headrest. If you look very closely at photogaphs of the 1840's and 1850's you can sometimes see the headrest that restrained the sitter.

A well-made daguerreotype preserves an image in great depth, richness, and detail. To distinguish a daguerreotype from other early photographs, hold the photograph in your hand and turn it first toward and then away from a source of light. If the image disappears into the mirrorlike finish, you can be sure that the photograph is a daguerreotype. This "disappearing image" was one of the least desirable features of the daguerreotype. Other drawbacks were the reversal of the image from right to left and the inability to make copies of a picture, since the process did not produce a negative from which prints could be produced.

By the 1850's photographers had developed new processes for creating both negatives and positive prints. The ambrotype, which became extremely popular for a short time in America (1854–1860's), was a negative image on glass that could be made to look like a positive by backing it with a black substance—velvet, varnish, paint, or paper. The tintype (1856–1890's), which was printed on metal rather than glass, was a more durable form of photograph. A uniquely American invention, patented in 1856 by Hamilton L. Smith, the tintype is actually misnamed. The picture was made not on tin but on the blackened surface of sheet iron. At first, a photograph made by this process was actually called a ferrotype, but soon the less accurate but more popular name tintype came into widespread use.

The tintype was much cheaper than the daguerreotype, and unlike the ambrotype it was unbreakable and could be carried about or sent through the mail. Its drawback, like that of the daguerreotype, was that a photographer could produce only one picture for each exposure. To overcome this difficulty, photographers sometimes used a multiple-lens camera to make more than one picture at the same time.

The development of paper prints in the 1850's enabled photographers to reproduce conveniently many pictures from a single negative. Albumen prints (1850's–1890's), which were produced on paper coated with egg white, were the most popular form of prints made in the mid and late nineteenth century. At first the photographer himself had to put the light-sensitive compounds on the paper used for prints, but later the paper could be bought already sensitized. One firm in Germany used 60,000 eggs a day to produce albumen paper for the European market. Considering the mechanical difficulties of early photography, one can imagine what a blessing this presensitized paper was to the photographer. Albumen prints were often mounted on cards used for the large cabinet prints (3¾ by 5½ inches). A great many of the photographs in your old albums will be cabinet cards of this type, dating primarily from 1860's through the 1890's.

The *carte de visite* (1854–1860's) was devised by the Duke of Parma, who wanted to use his photograph as his calling card. It was an interesting and immensely popular use of the albumen print. The Duke, who lived in France, had his photographer make small (2¼ by 3¾ inches) paper photographs, which were then pasted on his calling card.

By 1859 these *cartes de visite* were being manufactured in the United States, where Americans greeted them with great enthusiasm. The cards were cheaper than daguerreotypes and were easily sent through the mail. They made their appearance just as the Civil War was breaking out, and having one's picture taken "for the folks" before leaving for the army became a common practice. In no time at all, people were exchanging the cards at a fantastic rate. Indeed, the number of cards that many families collected became so great that a new kind of book became necessary to hold them—the photograph album. A *carte* of a famous person can be both rare and valuable. Your local history society may be able to help you identify any *carte de visite* if you think it may be the photograph of a celebrity. Family members often put pictures of themselves and famous people together into their albums, often without order or identification. Be alert when looking at these old albums; not every picture depicts a family member and some cards may have value.

It is difficult to distinguish albumen prints from more modern prints, but albumen prints do have some distinctive features. The paper is somewhat glossy but not as brilliantly glossy as the modern print. The highlights of an albumen print have a yellowish cast, and their color is light sepia rather than the black and white of today's pictures. A photograph which has these characteristics is likely to date from the nineteenth century. However, since nineteenth-century photographers experimented with many different kinds of methods, a photograph that appears to be of early twentieth century vintage might still have been produced in the nineteenth century.

Almost all photography in the twentieth century uses transparent and flexible celluloid film. Invented in 1888 by Hannibal Goodwin, an Episcopal minister from New Jersey, celluloid film is lightweight and unbreakable. It can be wound compactly upon a spool from which multiple exposures can safely be taken. A photographer could easily carry this film and snap his pictures without fear of accidental exposure.

In the same year that Goodwin invented celluloid film, the Eastman Kodak Company began the era of the amateur photogapher by introducing a small hand-held camera. Until 1888, the difficulty of taking and developing pictures meant that photography was primarily for the professional or the dedicated amateur. Now anyone could easily take pictures and let the company develop them.

The first Kodak cameras sold for twenty-five dollars. For this price one got a small boxlike camera with film already in place. Enough film was in the camera to take one hundred round pictures. (Rectangular Kodak pictures made their appearance in 1896.) The purchaser exposed the film and then sent the entire camera with the exposed film still inside to the Kodak Company. The company developed the film, inserted a new film into the camera, and returned the camera and pictures to the owner. The Kodak motto, "You push the button, we do the rest," became a household slogan, and the day of both the amateur and the snapshot had arrived.

The history of photography from 1888 until today is the story of ever-increasing ease of operation and greater sophistication for both the amateur and the professional. Films have become progressively more sensitive and shutter speeds progressively more rapid. Scientists and technicians have developed various kinds of equipment that allow the rankest amateur to produce sharp, clear pictures. They have also developed color prints and refined color film. Color prints in your family collection are not likely to date before the 1940's, and color slides before the mid-1930's.

In 1923, the Eastman Kodak Company also developed and marketed the first home movie camera. These cameras looked like large brownie cameras and used 16 mm film instead of the larger 35 mm film used by professionals. In 1932, Eastman Kodak brought out a camera that used the still more economical 8 mm film; thousands of families now began to make their own movies. Four years earlier, color movie film had appeared and eventually came to dominate the home movie market.

INTERPRETING PHOTOGRAPHS

The key question to ask in interpreting a photograph is simply "What suppositions about the past can explain why the picture looks the way it does?" But don't be fooled by the deceptive simplicity of this query. For every photograph is a product of three distinct inputs: the photographic process, the photographer, and the subjects. The camera is not simply a neutral instrument that records the world as it really is. The camera may not lie, but it also may not reveal what portion of the truth it is telling. The photographer exercises great control over the field of vision that the camera records. Not only does he decide what slice of the landscape to include within the borders of a photograph, but he may also instruct his human subjects and rearrange inanimate objects. Yet the options open to the photographer may be limited by different forms of equipment and technology. In addition, even when the photographer issues no instructions, people confronted with the lens of a camera may alter their ordinary appearance and behavior. So be very careful about concluding what historical realities are captured within the frames of your photographs.

DATING AND IDENTIFICATION

Before drawing any conclusions from your photographs, you should first devise a system for identifying each one of them. A simple yet reliable procedure is to assign code numbers to individual photographs. For ease of reference, you might have different numbering systems for pictures found in albums and for loose photographs. You might, for instance, number all of your albums A1, A2, A3, and so forth, and then number each picture sequentially as it appears in the album: A1–1, A1–2, A1–3, and so forth. Loose pictures can simply be numbered sequentially without any reference to an album number. A numbering scheme enables you to record information about photographs on separate file cards, each of which is labeled with the appropriate photograph number, and if you choose, with a descriptive title as well. This scheme also allows you to take pictures out of an album and easily return them to precisely the same place, preserving the album's historical integrity.

Try to identify the subjects, settings, and dates of each photograph. You might find that the back of a photograph or an entry in an album lists the names of the people depicted and the date of the photograph. You might even find some reference to the place where the photograph was taken and perhaps even to the occasion it portrays (for example, a vacation or a birthday party). When such information is recorded, photographs become valuable sources for discovering the names of ancestors and determining their whereabouts at various times. Indeed, people have used this kind of information to trace their lines of descent through as many as seven generations. But some or all of your photographs might contain no additional information whatever. You should then turn to family members to obtain as much information as possible.

You may find the name and location of the photographer stamped on the back or at the bottom of the photograph or card. Photohistorians are beginning to compile lists of the names of photographers from various cities and the dates during which they worked. These lists are particularly valuable for dating photographs taken in the nineteenth century.* To date the work of a photographer not in these lists, consult state and local historical societies, town records, or city business directories of the community in which the photograph was taken.

*The regional list of American photographers operating in the 1840's and 1850's in William Welling's *Collector's Guide to Nineteenth-Century Photographs* is extremely helpful. For a specialized list, see Richard Rudisill's *Photographers of the New Mexico Territory, 1854–1912* (Santa Fe: Museum of New Mexico, 1973).

With due caution you can also date a photograph or even identify subjects by simply looking at what the photograph portrays. For this task you will need both a knowledge of family background and a familiarity with the history of style, clothing, and material objects. Do you know when family members possessed an object, a home, or a parcel of land that might appear in a photograph? Can you date the models of automobiles or the types of home appliances? Do you know when men began wearing cuffs on their pants or women abandoned the hoop skirt? Even the most knowledgeable observers, however, can't always decide when a photograph was taken or whom it portrays. But don't discard unidentified and undated photographs; these pictures may still contain valuable information about family life.

ANALYSIS

Having identified your photographs as best you can, you are ready to draw out their stories. Like a written document or an oral interview, a photograph shouldn't be studied in isolation but should be used in conjunction with all other source material. Photographs do more than help you answer questions about the past. They offer you perhaps the most immediate and vivid impression of the past. The pictures that you see may fire your imagination, suggesting new areas to explore or new hunches to be considered in light of all the evidence. Seeing photographs of grandparents and their friends gathered about the dinner table during the early twentieth century might suggest a line of questions that you could ask about the visiting and entertaining practices of people from the old country who lived near one another in the United States.

Generally the more you know about a photograph, the more valuable it becomes as source material for family history. Where was the picture taken? What was going on at the time? Was someone present who isn't in the picture? Why was the picture taken? Was it taken by an amateur or a professional? Was the picture posed or spontaneous? Be careful to distinguish between the posed, formal photograph and the spontaneous snapshot. The photographer often controls the pose of a formal photograph and may even select the objects that appear in the picture. Yet formal photographs posed by the family itself may reveal much more about family life than a snapshot would. Whereas much information can often be teased from the analysis of a formal photograph, the effect of snapshots is cumulative.

Unless you are very careful and thoughtful in the analysis of photographs, you will likely leap to erroneous conclusions. For example, you might find a photograph of your great-great-grandfather taken in the 1840's. Without knowing much about photography you might speculate about his personality from his still, stern appearance in the photograph. But we know that the photographic process in the 1840's generally required people to sit for several minutes clamped in an uncomfortable chair. Does your ancestor's appearance reflect his rigid personality or simply the procedure used to take his photograph? Similarly, you might find a photograph of a family standing very close together. Does this pose mean that the family was very close emotionally, or does it mean only that a photographer asked people to move close together in order to accommodate his tastes and the capacity of his camera?

In a study of early pictures, Richard Rudisill offers yet another explanation for the characteristically stiff and formal poses. For people of the 1840's, he argues, the preservation of their likeness was not a commonly accepted part of life. Rather, having a photograph taken gave to individuals a sense of importance once reserved only for those who could afford to commission a painted portrait. According to Rudisill, the subject of an early photograph was solemn, erect, and reserved because he was representing himself both as an individual person and as an American.

To aid in the interpretation of photographs, you should consult books about photography to learn the photographic conventions of the times when your photographs were taken. Professional historians are now just beginning to identify the conventions and standards of formal photographs. By consulting relevant literature, you can acquire knowledge helpful in interpreting your own pictures. Study the pictures and commentary in published work on photographic history until you begin to get a feel for what photographs from a particular time were like. If, for example, a great many photographs show men posing with their hands on a Bible, you should not jump to the conclusion that the Bible meant a great deal to these people. Be careful to differentiate, if it's possible, between convention and personal expression.

If you decide that family members probably chose the pose, the setting, and the objects of a formal photograph, you can ask yourself why these ancestors made the choices that they did. Look at how people use the space around them, at the setting in which they appear, at the material objects portrayed in the photograph. How do people position themselves in relation to each other? Do they hold hands or touch in some other way? Who is sitting and who is standing? Where was the photograph taken—in the kitchen, in the living room, or in front of the house? Are people holding any small objects? Are they posed next to pieces of furniture or other items? What objects appear in the background? What kind of clothing are they wearing? You might, for example, speculate that a family photographed when standing apart might be following a family or cultural tradition that people didn't touch one another. You might conjecture that a woman posed in the kitchen might attach great significance to her role as cook and homemaker, or that a farmer portrayed holding a team of horses hitched to a plow might closely identify with his work horses. You might surmise that a photograph of a woman holding a picture of a dead relative suggests that she had strong positive feelings about the dead person. In each case, of course, you would look for other evidence relevant to determining the truth of your hunches.

Don't discard photographs because they portray conventional poses and objects. Remember that every bit of historical evidence was produced in response to something that happened in the past. Your job is to figure out what in the past accounts for the evidence that you observe in the present. A family seeking higher status, for instance, might try to pose as the rich and the famous did. A family might pose on their large lawn because they want to show that they are wealthy enough to have such a lawn. A family might dress in certain clothes because they believe that these clothes are the best fashion of the times. Generally people are inclined to show the camera what they hope will convince others to think well of them.

If you have formal photographs from more than one generation of family history, compare them. Look at the photographs to see what has changed. Differences in how families are portrayed may reflect changes in family life as well as changes in photographic convention. In the photographs of David Challinor's family, his grandfather, John D. Crimmins, was always the center of any picture taken between 1890 and 1920. But in the generation of his grandfather's daughter she, not her husband, was always in the center. These photos show clearly what other evidence also confirms: that there was a striking change from a patriarchal to a matriarchal family in a single generation. Family members attribute this change to the sheer force of character of the daughter.

Snapshots are unposed photographs usually taken by an amateur, often when the subjects are completely unaware that they are being photographed. In these cases, the camera becomes a device for stopping time and movement as it naturally occurs. At other times people may have an opportunity to pose quickly before a snapshot is taken. Perhaps they have a chance to run a comb through their hair, smooth their clothing, and compose their features. Even snapshots taken under these circumstances, however, are not the product of the elaborate planning that goes into a formal, posed photograph.

A few photographs taken in the 1800's could qualify as snapshots, although the heavy equipment and difficult developing process discouraged amateur photography. The day of the snapshot began in the late 1880's, with the invention of the hand-held Kodak camera. As the exposure time for film became shorter, the snapshot increased in popularity, becoming widespread by the beginning of the 1920's.

Some experts in photography argue that snapshots capture a "truer" slice of life than the posed photograph. Certainly snapshots are more spontaneous than formal portraits and show a greater variety of situations. But the very spontaneity of snapshots limits the insight they offer into family history. The subjects of a snapshot were less likely than those who posed for a formal picture to have carefully selected the relationship of people to one another, the setting for the photograph, and the objects that are portrayed. And even in a snapshot the photographer himself may have exercised some control over whom he decided to photograph and what activities or poses he chose to capture.

A striking advantage of snapshots as a source for family history is that families usually own hundreds of them spanning several decades of time. Because snapshots can be taken anywhere, they may be useful means of learning the family's whereabouts at various times. Moreover, snapshots can be used to reconstruct a cross section of family history at a particular time or to reveal changes over time in the nature of family life.

A group of folklorists at the Smithsonian Institution have carefully studied the modern photograph album.

Looking at thousands of snapshots in hundreds of albums, these folklorists have found that snapshots usually portray events rather than everyday life. The same kinds of events show up repeatedly in family albums: vacations, graduations, holidays, birthdays, bar mitzvahs, weddings. Even the same poses are likely to turn up in the snapshots of different families: the family grouped on the front porch steps, the owner of a new car in the 1930's with one foot on the running board, children playing in plastic pools in the backyard, the graduate standing between proud parents. The events recorded in modern snapshots tend to be happy events. People are fashioning their own history in photographs and seem inclined to record pleasant rather than sad times. People don't generally photograph funerals, tearful partings, and sick people.

These findings mean that you shouldn't expect snapshots to disclose all facets of family life. In leafing through photograph albums you aren't likely to reconstruct the day-to-day lives of family members. Neither are you likely to unearth people's fears, failures, tragedies, or misfortunes.

Albums of the late nineteenth century, however, generally present at least one startling contrast to those compiled more recently. People looking at albums of the 1890's have frequently encountered pictures of children who seem to be asleep. In fact, these children were dead. At the end of the nineteenth century, parents often photographed deceased children both in and out of their coffins. People also photographed adults lying in their coffins, sometimes with the funeral party included in the picture.

Historians have argued that this distinction between the albums of today and those of the 1890's can be explained by changing attitudes toward death. In the late nineteenth century, these historians suggest, people were willing to accept and record the death of loved ones as a normal and natural part of life. They didn't avoid and deny the reality of death as we seem to do in contemporary America.

Consider your own albums and collections in the light of this finding. Do striking changes appear in snapshots taken by members of your family at different periods of time? What changes in your family or in the broader society can account for what you observe in the snapshots? What other evidence can be marshaled to judge the truth of what you surmise?

Another useful technique for interpreting snapshots is to arrange them by theme, situation, or individual and then chronologically within each group. There are many classification schemes you can follow. You can put together all pictures showing an event of a certain kind, such as a wedding, a bar mitzvah, or a Christmas dinner. You could also assemble all pictures showing a common object—a car or a house, for example. Among other possibilities, you could also put together all pictures in which a member of the family appears, thus creating an informal photographic biography. Each time you reshuffle the pictures you should be able to learn something new about your family history. If you have numbered each photograph according to an orderly scheme you can rearrange them without worrying about replacing them in the family albums.

Once your pictures are arranged by subject and date, you can see the patterns they form. You may observe that things change gradually over time or remain pretty much the same. You may also find that change takes place in sudden leaps or seems random with respect to time, following no simple chronological pattern. Snapshots may even reveal family members reverting to the styles and practices of an earlier time.

Look at wedding pictures, for example. Do the weddings portrayed seem to be religious or social events or perhaps a combination of the two? Are weddings becoming more or less formal? What role does food seem to play in different weddings? Do the poses of the members of the wedding party change over time? Are there ritual poses that appear repeatedly? Is the minister or rabbi part of the wedding party, or does he appear only in the role of outsider or guest? Is there a difference in the pictures taken by a professional photographer as opposed to a family member? Moreover, try to find out if there have been weddings at which no photographs were taken. If not, why not? The number of questions you can ask is limited only by the scope of your imagination and by the time you want to give the project.

You can analyze home movies through the same methods used to study still photographs. But remember that movies add the additional element of motion. The ways in which people move may tell you something about their physical vitality, their personalities, and even their relationships with one another. One student, for instance, arrived at a new understanding of what her grandmother was like by viewing a home movie taken in the 1930's. The film showed her grandmother, then a woman of twenty-five, race out the front door of her house, hurdle the porch fence, and turn three quick cartwheels on the front lawn.

Every family historian can profitably exploit the evidence of photographs and home movies. Even a single photograph can bring an immediacy to perceptions of your family history that no historical document can. Professional historians are also beginning to appreciate the unique value of photographic evidence. Herbert Gutman writes in the introduction to his book on the history of the black family: "The most important single piece of historical evidence in this book is neither an isolated statistic, a historical 'anecdote,' a numerical table or chart. It is the photograph that adorns the jacket of this book and serves as its frontispiece." The photograph shows five generations of a black slave family gathered together at one time. It confirms that this black family was not fragmented by slavery but kept its identity throughout the centuries during which its members were enslaved. The picture lends reality to the bare names recorded in plantation records. It is indeed the most important historical document in the book.

Chapter 6

SOURCES OUTSIDE THE HOME

MANY FAMILY HISTORIANS will want to venture beyond the home and trace their ancestry in libraries, archives, and other repositories of records. Most of these records haven't been published, but are preserved by a governmental or private organization. But don't ignore such published sources as family genealogies, local histories, and newspapers. Sources found outside the home may offer only snippets of information. One record might yield the maiden name of a great-grandmother, another the date of her birth, and another the cause of her death. But outside sources may be the only way to gather information about your more distant ancestors. These records may also be vital for verifying information acquired from other sources. The family historian on the trail of elusive documents experiences the excitement of detective work and eventually the satisfaction of discovering a great-grandmother's name in a dusty registry of marriage licenses or an application for a Western homestead filled out in the hand of a great-great-grandfather.

If you decide to use outside records, carefully plan your research, because there are many different sources of information. These include records produced by every level of government, documents produced by churches and private organizations (schools, businesses, and clubs), and published work in both history and genealogy, which will help you fill in gaps in your research.

STATE AND LOCAL RECORDS

The Constitution of the United States reserves for "the states and the people" all powers "not delegated to the federal government." Throughout most of our history, the state and local governments have been most directly concerned with the daily lives of Americans, thereby creating many useful records. Indeed, until the American Revolution there was no central government on American soil. The states and localities have been responsible for keeping track of births, marriages, deaths, and land transactions. They have established public schools, supervised elections, and maintained public health and safety. Local administrators have collected taxes, and local courts have handled most civil and criminal cases, including divorces and the probate of wills. The states and their localities have also had welfare responsibilities for the orphaned, the indigent, the ill, and the insane.

State and local records may contain information on ancestors that is available from no other sources. But locating these records requires knowledge, patience, and powers of deduction. Uniform procedures for collecting and preserving records do not prevail from one state to the next. New England town governments, for instance, began recording information on births and deaths early in the seventeenth century, but governments in the Southern states often lagged more than two centuries behind. In frontier territories records of all kinds were kept haphazardly, if at all. Documents that once existed may no longer exist anywhere due to neglect, fire, weather, insects, and other hazards. Some of the records you seek may be located in a town hall of records or a county courthouse; others may be available at a central repository like a state library or archive. Some records will be restricted by confidentiality laws; others will not. Sometimes you can obtain records by mail; other times you will have to visit the relevant respository in person. Some of the officials you encounter will be helpful and friendly, but others may be surly, uninterested, and anxious to send you on your way.

VITAL RECORDS

"Birth, and copulation, and death," observed Sweeney of T. S. Eliot's "Sweeney Agonistes," "that's all the facts when you come to brass tacks." Vital records refer to the documents that report people's births, deaths, and marriages. These records may be your only reliable source for determining the dates and places of these benchmarks in the history of ancestors. But vital records offer much more to the enterprising researcher.

Although the nature of vital records varies according to time and place, they usually share some common features. Birth records usually include a person's full name, the date and place of his birth, and the names of his parents. Especially for the period following 1900, they may also indicate the legitimacy of the birth; the ages of the parents, their races, and their places of birth; the person attending the birth; and previous births by the mother. State and local governments have created many different kinds of marriage records, including marriage licenses, returns reporting facts of the marriage, entries in registers, and in early periods, declarations of the intention to marry (do not assume, however, that marriage necessarily followed such declarations). Marriage records generally offer the names of the bride and groom, their ages, and the date and the location of the wedding. They are invaluable sources for the maiden names of female ancestors. (Do you know the maiden names of even your grandmothers?) Sometimes marriage records may also include data on race, religion, parental consent, occupation, and previous marital history. When available, death records are likely to offer considerable information: the cause of a person's death; his name, age, occupation, place and date of birth, place and date of death; the names and birthplaces of his parents; the date and place of burial; and the names and addresses of the informant and the undertaker. Remember, however, that death certificates were often composed hastily with information from grieving relatives and that medical theory and practice have changed substantially since the late nineteenth century.

Most states didn't adopt laws governing the registration of vital statistics until the late nineteenth or early twentieth century. Prior to this time, record collection and storage was usually left to localities; some kept good records from an early period, while others kept no records at all. Fortunately for today's researchers, unemployed intellectuals working for the Works Progress Administration (WPA) during the 1930's produced guides to the availability of vital records in the counties, towns, and cities of forty states. You can find these guides at major libraries or state historical societies.* In a few states (primarily in New England, where the tradition of keeping accurate records was most firmly established), early vital records are compiled and collected at the state library or archive.

For the period following the adoption of statewide registration laws, access to records is much easier. In most cases the appropriate state office will even conduct a search for records if you supply a name and the approxi-

*See Sargent B. Child and Dorothy P. Holmes, *Check List of Historical Records Survey Publications: Bibliography of Research Project Reports* (reprinted by Genealogical Publishing Co., Baltimore, 1969).

mate date of a birth, death, or marriage. Be aware, however, that access to birth records is usually restricted to the subject of the record, and his parents or legal guardians. Although death and marriage records are less likely to be encumbered with restrictions, some states still require authorization before releasing information. A series of pamphlets published by the federal government tells where to write for various types of vital records and the fees charged by state governments: "Where to Write for Birth and Death Records," "Where to Write for Marriage Records," and "Where to Write for Births and Deaths of U.S. Citizens Who Were Born or Died Outside of the United States and Birth Certificates for Alien Children Adopted by U.S. Citizens." You can purchase them for a nominal fee from the Superintendent of Documents, U.S. Government Printing Office, Washington, D.C. 20402. In *Building an American Pedigree* (pp. 564–598), Norman E. Wright has a useful section on vital records that goes beyond the government pamphlets to indicate (as of publication time) the confidentiality of records, fees for searches as well as for copies of documents, and policies regarding the searches that state officials will perform.

PROBATE RECORDS

"Ah! If I were rich," sighs the dying Père Goriot of Balzac's novel, "if I'd kept my money and never given it to them, they'd be here now, licking my cheeks with their kisses! . . . If I had money to leave, they'd be nursing me and looking after me." Whenever a person dies and leaves an estate, records are created that may reveal much about how he lived. Probate is the process by which a court of proper jurisdiction apportions a person's estate after his death. Probate will usually take place if a deceased person had wealth or possessions, regardless of whether he left a will. An estate is termed "testate" if a will exists and is validated by the court. If no will is found or no will is approved, the estate is then considered "intestate" and is distributed according to state law. Wills submitted to the court along with other documents created in the legal proceedings become part of the official record.

Gilbert H. Doane, author of *Searching for Your Ancestors* (for several decades the standard introduction to genealogy), wrote that "undoubtedly the most important evidence of the genealogy of a family is a collection of the probate court records which pertain to it." For the family historian as well as for the genealogist, these records may indeed be plentiful sources of information. The wills of individuals may be written or verbal (remember that many people have had difficulty with the written word); they may range in length from a single sentence to many thousands of words (one lengthy will was bound into four separate volumes). Even the briefest of wills may tell you something about a family. The silent President Calvin Coolidge revealed something about himself and his family in a one-sentence will: "Not unmindful of my son John, I give all my estate both real and personal to my wife Grace Coolidge, in fee simple." Wills may provide information about many aspects of family life. The more comprehensive of wills may name descendants, relatives, and friends, indicating their relationship to the deceased. A will may disclose a person's occupation, his place of birth and places of residence, his religious affiliation, and his financial and social status. It may also reveal something of his tastes and style of life, his relationships with other family members, his political preferences, or his favorite charities and causes. Often witnesses named in the will were close personal friends of the deceased (beneficiaries of a will can't also be witnesses). A researcher might find that the mysterious "Uncle Bill" was really William Bunch, a boyhood friend of the deceased ancestor.

Along with wills, other revealing documents may be part of a probate file. Petitions for probate often include the date and place of the person's death, and the names and addresses of all known heirs to the estate. In earlier times, even when one parent survived, the court may have assigned guardians for minor children, generating records with data about the children, about the guardian, and sometimes about the circumstances of family life. An executor or administrator of a will may inventory, appraise, and ultimately auction off the property of the deceased, creating invaluable economic records. Contested wills may bring grief and bitterness to a family, but they may yield bounties of information to the family historian. Even if only one individual (who must be a relative) contested a will, most state courts require as many friends and relatives as possible to submit depositions. In addition, the court will generally issue a report of how an estate was finally apportioned, frequently naming each heir and indicating their relationship to the deceased.

Intestate proceedings may also yield informative records. In effect, when a person dies without a legally approved will, the government writes a will for him, according to a formula which apportions his assets among the heirs. (Estates without valid wills may also be inventoried, appraised, and sold at auction.) Records of the court hearing on an intestate estate may include much testimony from individuals claiming to be relatives of the deceased, especially if the estate is substantial. Eventually the court will issue a report about the distribution to contestants.

The more you know about local law and custom, the better you will be able to interpret probate records. These documents may be laced with technical terms and legal phrases that have precise definitions. *Black's Law Dictionary* is the standard reference for legal terminology, but be alert to variation from state to state. Relationships within a family can sometimes be deduced from the form or context of a probate record. In some places, people have typically listed their sons and daughters in order of birth. For intestate proceedings, familiarity with state law can disclose the court's judgment of relationships, since each type of relative (wife, son, daughter, and so forth), will be granted a fixed proportion of the estate.

Probate records are considered valuable partly because they have been carefully preserved and are available for most periods of American history. Probate records are usually in the custody of clerks of the appropriate courts, located in each county of a state. In *Building an American Pedigree* (pp. 599–627), Norman Wright describes the probate holdings of each state. Copies of many local wills have been made and then stored in central repositories within the states. These copies, however, must be used with care, since errors can creep into the copying process. Moreover, some copies may be abstracts or summaries of the will's content, whereas others may be extracts, or exact copies of the wills.

LAND RECORDS

A few of the early immigrants to North America came in search of gold and precious gems. Others sought the opportunity to practice their form of religion or to escape the gallows and the prison cell. But rich and abundant land was the main lure for settlement in the New World. Since the first colonists divided land among themselves, Americans have conducted and recorded countless land transactions. Many of the records created throughout American history are still accessible to you. In the years when America was overwhelmingly a land of farmers, most males owned land at some point in their lives.

Land records useful to the family historian are created primarily when a unit of government transfers land to an individual or when people sell or lease land to one another. The most notable of these records are deeds (the documents by which land was transferred from one party to another), mortgages, leases, and records of state government grants (primarily useful for colonial America, these records may take many forms depending upon the time and the place). Other land records often filed in the same place include bills of sale, notes of land transfer, surveyor's records, rent rolls, power of attorney, and other agreements among individuals. Deeds and records of land grants will usually include the names, residences (and often occupations and spouse's names of parties to the transaction), the monetary terms of the transaction, any limitations, restrictions or reservations regarding the land, the date of the deed and the recording, and the names of witnesses. Records of land given in return for military service include the branch of service, the dates of service, and the residence of the applicant while his claim for land was processed. Family relationships may also be indicated in land records, as well as odd tidbits of information about the family.

Most land records are located in the county in which the transaction took place (or the town for the New England states of Connecticut, New Hampshire, Rhode Island, and Vermont). In *The Check List of Historical Records Survey Publications,* Child and Holmes provide brief descriptions of the holdings of local agencies. As with other local documents, some land records have also been copied and sent to the state archive or library. With some exceptions these records usually are indexed by the names of both the buyers and the sellers and are open to the public. For a fee, the custodians of land records may be willing to search these indexes for you and duplicate the appropriate records. But don't expect officials to perform full-scale research into the many land records that may mention one of your ancestors.

The family historian who searches for land records enters an especially dense thicket of legal terminology. Do you know, for example, the meaning of such commonly used terms as "quitclaim," "section," "plat," and "conveyance?" One beginning researcher became very frustrated after spending several hours looking for the deed to an ancestor's property. He solved his problem only after being told that deeds were also known as conveyances. Reexamining the land records, he quickly found the conveyance he was looking for. Before plunging into land records read the descriptions in Wright, *Building an American Pedigree,* (pp. 233–277), and Val D. Greenwood, *The Researcher's Guide to American Genealogy* (pp. 264–315), and be ready to consult *Black's Law Dictionary.* When properly understood, land records can yield information not only about relationships but also about movement from place to place, occupation, and financial standing.

OTHER COURT RECORDS

Americans seem always to have been a litigious people, continually bringing their disputes to courts for resolution. In 1815, for instance, Benjamin Rush wrote that "the habits, the manners, and the contentions of the universally thriving and self-supporting freemen on this side of the Atlantic call for at least a couple of lawyers . . . where the English do for one." Many details of family history may be buried in the records of civil and even of criminal courts. Court records are among the most carefully preserved documents of the state and local government, and they may include abundant information.

Most court records, like divorce documents, are obviously germane to a study of family history. Certificates of divorce, issued by most but not all states, usually provide the names of the parties, the wedding date, and the date of the divorce. To check the availability of divorce certificates, you can purchase "Where to Write for Divorce Records, United States and Outlying Areas," from the Superintendent of Documents. The actual court records of divorce cases will contain much more information, including the names and ages of dependent children, dates and places of birth for both parties, the grounds for divorce, and the property settlement, if any. Records of contested divorces may also include detailed, if sad and troubling, testimony about family life. Most divorce records are indexed and available to the public. If you know the name of one of the parties and the approximate year of the divorce you usually can obtain the record, with payment of a fee, from the appropriate court. In *The Researcher's Guide* (pp. 345–346), Greenwood lists the court of jurisdiction for each state.

If you can identify ancestors born outside the United States, you will want to look for records of their naturalization as American citizens (keeping in mind, of course, that not every alien sought naturalization). Naturalization records may bridge the ocean for you, revealing the Old World homeland of an ancestor. They may also be the only written records available for an immigrant ancestor. Prior to the standardization of naturalization procedures by federal law in 1906, naturalization could take place in any federal, state, or local court. Although state naturalization records vary in content, most will include your ancestor's name, the date and place of residence at the time of application, whether citizenship was granted, and sometimes the person's occupation and the ship on which he arrived in the United States.

Access to naturalization records dated before standardization usually requires identification of the court that conducted the proceedings. Moreover, between 1855 and the passage of the Cable Act in 1922, a woman automatically became a citizen when she married a citizen or her husband became naturalized. Thus most naturalization records for this period will be for male ancestors. In a few cases naturalization records located within states have been duplicated and centralized for convenient reference. During the 1930's the WPA indexed and copied naturalization records for Maine, Massachusetts, New Hampshire, Rhode Island, and Vermont. The indexes and the copies of the New England records are available at the National Archives and Records Service in Washington, D.C. Information for New York City is at the Federal Records Center at Bayonne, New Jersey. Federal employees will search these indexes for you, but federal law forbids the duplication of a naturalization record; only abstracts can be made. The WPA has also prepared guides to naturalization records located in Mississippi and New Jersey, and there are alphabetized lists of naturalization records for Baltimore from 1833 to 1866 and Boston from 1848 to 1891.

If you are aware of other legal proceedings involving your ancestors, you might find it rewarding to look up the records. The proceedings of a property dispute might shed light on the tension between your grandfather and his "damned neighbor." Suits for the payment of debt might disclose the financial dealings of your great-grandfather. Criminal prosecutions and hearings for civil commitment might reveal the deeds of that horse thief in your family or disclose the plight of an ancestor who was mentally ill. Most civil court cases are indexed according to the names of both plaintiff and defendant and criminal court cases according to the name of the accused.

STATE CENSUS REPORTS

Every ten years we are reminded that the federal government conducts a census of the population. But many people are not aware that from time to time state governments also have taken censuses of various kinds. Rapidly expanding territories surveyed their population to qualify for statehood. States also conducted censuses for such special purposes as tallying the number of the insane within their borders. State census records are generally located in state archives, but some censuses, especially those taken in the territories, have been microfilmed and deposited in the National Archives. For a discussion of state census records, see the dated but still useful government pamphlet *State Censuses: An Annotated Bibliography of Censuses of Population Taken After the Year 1790 by States and Territories in the United States.* You can also consult the more recent *Census Compendium,* published in 1972 by the Gendex Corporation of Salt Lake City.

TAX RECORDS

Proving again that death and taxes are constants of life, governments have taxed Americans since the founding of the Colonies. As a family historian you will be interested in lists of those who paid taxes on real estate, on personal property, or on both. These lists can serve as a census of taxpayers in a town, helping you locate ancestors and trace their movements from one place to another. Along with census schedules they can help re-create the social and economic character of an ancestor's community. They may supply you with the data to learn the size and value of an ancestor's farm or to trace the economic history of a family over time. Records of personal property taxes are especially valuable because they include people who didn't own land. Finding tax records can be a hit-or-miss affair, since many governments didn't keep good tax records in their early years; usually you will have to look for these records in the registries of local governments. Before interpreting the records that you do find, be sure that you know the criteria by which property was assessed for purposes of taxation. Was real estate, for example, assessed at full market value or at some percentage of the market value?

OTHER STATE AND LOCAL RECORDS

The list of records mentioned thus far does not yet exhaust the compendium of state and local records available to the family historian. Some records of early public schools and public welfare agencies still survive. Election records from the nineteenth and very early twentieth century may list individual voters by name. And states have kept records of those who served in the militia or worked for the state government. Southern states also have valuable Confederate records. When researching state and local sources, try to visit both state and local repositories of records. No guidebook of family history can detail what you might find through personal research in a state archive, a town hall, or a county courthouse.

FEDERAL RECORDS

Although the federal government has been less involved in the lives of individuals than the states and their localities, events of your ancestors' lives may have brought them in touch with the federal government and created records for you to exploit. Was a great-great-grandfather drafted to serve in the Civil War? Did a grandmother pass through federal customs at Ellis Island? Did an ancestor apply for a federal pension, request a passport, seek land in the public domain, or work for the federal government? Since 1790 the federal government has regularly conducted a decennial census of the population, and in some years, a census of mortality as well.

Research in federal records is generally more orderly and serene than the exploration of state and local sources. Virtually all important records are located in the National Archives and Records Service and its eleven regional branches throughout the country. An imposing building of classical style just off the mall in Washington, D.C., the National Archives is the repository for official records of the federal government. There professional historians pore over reports of the Department of Justice, photographs of the world wars, and despatches of American ambassadors. There, too, many researchers have achieved thrilling breakthroughs in family history. Archives officials report that the great majority of their users are researching family history. The family history resources of the archives and its branches are thoroughly inventoried and described in the forbidding but comprehensive *Guide to Genealogical Records in the National Archives* by Bill R. Linder and James D. Walker. This forthcoming work is a revised and updated version of an earlier guide published in 1964. Readers should be aware that the guide thoroughly describes sources but doesn't tell you how to perform genealogical research.

CENSUS AND MORTALITY SCHEDULES

If your lineage in the United States goes back to the nineteenth century, schedules of the federal census are indispensable sources of family history. These census reports for individual households list people by name and, after 1840, include personal data of various kinds. Census schedules are open to researchers for censuses taken from 1790 to 1900. To preserve people's privacy, later schedules are closed by statute law. Through special request to the Bureau of the Census you can obtain information about yourself from schedules after 1900 or information about a deceased person if you were a member of his immediate family (spouse, parent, child, brother, or sister) or a beneficiary with legal proof of this status.

Responding to a constitutional mandate that the government enumerate the population to apportion direct taxes and representation in Congress, federal officials conducted the first decennial census in 1790.* The first census listed by name only the head of the household and simply noted his place of residence and the number of people in the household (divided into age and sex categories). This precedent was closely followed until the census of 1850, when the census marshals listed the name, age, and sex of every free member of a household. The census reports for

*The government has also conducted various special censuses, not necessarily in the regular census years.

1850 and 1860 include separate schedules that list slaves by age, sex, and color, but not by name. Although the government did not record the same information in each census, the schedules from 1850 to 1900 also offer a range of information about family members, including literacy, place of birth, occupation, value of real estate, and such physical impairments as blindness and deafness. Census schedules may supply information not available elsewhere and may enable you to learn something about the communities in which your ancestors lived. The families living near your ancestor will usually be listed on the same census roll. With persistence and luck a researcher might be able to trace family lines over time, identifying births and deaths in a family or detecting changes in family structure. A family historian might be able to see if a person changed his occupation or if children followed the occupation of their parents. Linder and Walker's *Guide to Genealogical Records* has a complete listing of information available from each census.

You can consult census schedules at the National Archives or one of its regional branches. You can also turn to the library of the Church of the Latter-Day Saints and its many branches for microfilm copies of the census through 1880. Microfilms of census schedules dated prior to 1900 can also be found at other major libraries throughout the nation. You can also purchase microfilm rolls of census schedules from the National Archives. See the National Archives publication *Federal Population Censuses 1790–1890* for order forms and a complete list of available rolls.

Census schedules are organized first by state, then by county, then by minor civil division, and finally the entries by surname. Thus to search feasibly for the listing of an ancestor, you will already have to know the state and county (or ward if a city resident) in which he resided when the census marshals made their rounds. Ideally you will want to know the town and the street address as well, particularly if the county or city is very populous. (Remember too that the boundary lines of counties and cities have changed over time.) Only the first census of 1790 is fully indexed and published, with copies available at many major libraries. The ubiquitious WPA also indexed the census schedules for 1880 and 1900, first by state and then by family name. To adjust for the many variant spellings of the same family name, the surnames in these indexes are arranged according to the Soundex system. The names are listed alphabetically by the first letter and then by a numerical code designed to keep together names with similar sounds. The 1880 index is only for families with children ten years and younger. The 1900 index includes the surnames of all household heads with cross-references for each person in the household with a different last name from that of the head.

Despite their obvious value for family history, census records have their shortcomings. Census reports are not complete enumerations of the population; even today the census misses people at random and consistently undercounts such groups as poor people and racial minorities. Veterans of census research also tell the story of the "missing corner house." It seems that a group of census marshals continually "missed" the house on the corner, each thinking that it was the responsibility of another worker. Also, the informant (sometimes deliberately) or the census taker may have been careless with the spelling of names. The census schedules for a given year may spell even a common name like "Franklin" in more than a dozen different ways. And people may be listed by both given names and nicknames. One student spent weeks searching for a Robert Joyner in the census of 1870. Only after looking instead for "Doc" Joyner was he eventually able to find the ancestor. So don't assume that information locating an ancestor in a particular county during a census year is wrong simply because the person cannot be found in the census schedules. And don't assume that a person must have moved out of a county simply because his name disappears from one census to the next.

The listing of people with the same name or with variant spellings of a name that could be the same greatly complicates the search for ancestors in census reports. The problem is especially vexing when using the state-by-state indexes of 1880 and 1900; you may find dozens of people with the same soundex code and first name as the ancestor you seek. Unless you had additional information such as the name of a spouse or a date of birth you would be unable to choose among these prospective candidates for your family tree. Indeed, the same problem may arise even if you know the place of residence, since several people from the same county or even the same town may have approximately the same name. In short, you can use the census schedules most effectively when you already possess some basic information about your forebears.

Even when you can locate an ancestor and his family, question the accuracy of census data. By mistake or by design, people may have fed false information to the census taker knocking at their door (in the nineteenth century census marshals sometimes were regarded as akin to tax collectors). Even under the best of circumstances, people aren't reliable reporters of some types of information. For instance, individuals are so likely to misstate their ages that historians have used computations of age bias in census reports as evidence of changing attitudes toward the aging process itself (are people consistently biasing their age upward or downward?). Census takers without much education or anxious to complete their rounds may have misrecorded information or even concocted data when families were difficult to reach.

Finally, there are gaps in the census records. Fire has destroyed virtually all census schedules for 1890, and scattered schedules are likewise missing for earlier years as well. Some census schedules are illegible. Prior to 1880, census reports don't identify household members by their relationship to the household head. Thus children listed on a census form could have been nephews and nieces or sons and daughters. Other data do not appear consistently on the census schedules. To the chagrin of anyone studying social mobility in a family, the population census only recorded the value of personal property in 1860 and 1870 and the value of real estate in 1850, 1860, and 1870.

From 1850 to 1880 the federal censuses also included mortality schedules that listed the individuals who died in the year preceding the census, indicating the month in which they died, the cause of their death, and the state, territory, or foreign country in which they were born. The National Archives is attempting to microfilm all the mortality schedules, but the task is still not complete. The Archives has schedules for Arizona, Colorado, District of Columbia, Delaware, Georgia, Illinois, Kansas, Kentucky, Louisiana, Massachusetts, Minnesota, Montana, Nebraska, New Jersey, North Carolina, North Dakota, South Carolina, Tennessee, Texas, Utah, Vermont, Virginia, and Washington. The library of the National Society of the Daughters of the American Revolution also has an extensive collection of mortality schedules. Other schedules are located in various state archives and libraries.

PASSENGER ARRIVAL LISTS

Any family historian might strike pure gold by locating a report recording the arrival of an ancestor from abroad. The two most important types of passenger arrival records are the customs passenger lists and immigration passenger lists. A ship's master prepared the customs passenger lists, usually recording the name of the vessel and master, the port of departure, the date and port of arrival, as well as the name, sex, occupation, country of origin, and country of destination for each passenger. The content of the immigration passenger lists varies according to date and place. By 1893 standard forms included the name of each passenger; his age, sex, marital status, occupation, last legal residence, port of arrival, and final destination in the United States; whether he had been in the United States before; whether he was going to join a relative; and if so, the relative's name, address, and relationship to the passenger. Later, the lists were again revised to include information on race, birthplace, personal description, and nearest relative in the country of origin. Both types of lists would also include reports of both births and deaths that occurred en route.

The National Archives has incomplete lists of passenger arrivals primarily from 1820 to 1945. Although many of the earlier records no longer survive, you might find it worthwhile to check *A Bibliography of Ship Passenger Lists, 1538–1825,* by Harold Lancour and revised by R. J. Wolfe. For the more recent era, fire destroyed most lists for San Francisco,* the Archives doesn't have lists for other West Coast ports, and data for New York between 1847 and 1896 is missing. During the nineteenth century the government didn't require records to be kept for those arriving by land from Canada or Mexico. Despite such omissions, if your ancestor entered the United States at a major East Coast port after 1820, the odds are pretty good that a record of his arrival still exists. But actually laying hands on a passenger arrival list may be quite difficult. Only lists more than fifty years old may be examined by researchers; all others are closed by confidentiality laws. Although most of the unrestricted lists are indexed, these indexes generally are arranged by port, by year, and then by name of vessel. This means that to avoid an interminable search through columns of names you will need to know the port of entry for an ancestor, the vessel on which he sailed, and the approximate date of his arrival. Knowledge of an exact arrival date and the port of depar-

*Louis J. Rasmussen is now in the process of reconstructing these lists and has produced several volumes of his *Ship 'N Rail* series.

ture can also substitute for knowledge of the vessel's name. If you can acquire the necessary information from oral history, naturalization records, or other documents, employees of the Archives will search the indexes and for a small fee will send you copies of an ancestor's record. Any information that you have about an ancestor's arrival can be supplemented with *The Morton Allan Directory of European Passenger Steamship Arrivals,* which lists by year, company, and exact date the arrival of vessels in New York between 1890 and 1930, and in Baltimore, Boston, and Philadelphia, between 1904 and 1926.

When searching for passenger arrival records, be alert to that odd spelling of a name. The communications gap between immigrants and officials is enshrined in the folklore of many families. In 1887, Vittorio San Giacomo arrived in the port of New York. The customs official recording his entry spelled Vittorio San Giacomo as it sounded, listing Tony San Jachimo on the official record. Unless this story had been handed down in the family or the researcher had persistently checked all possible spellings of Vittorio San Giacomo, the passenger arrival record would never have been found. Communication problems may lead to errors and inaccuracies in other information included on passenger arrival lists too.

MILITARY RECORDS

Before the era of the cold war between West and East, the United States maintained only a small force of regular soldiers in times of peace. But the wars that punctuate every generation of American history have called for the mustering of hundreds of thousands or even millions of volunteers and draftees. The National Archives has the service records of those who served in wars and insurrections (1775–1902, including draft and other records from the Civil War) from the Revolutionary War to the Philippine Insurrection. Through the late nineteenth and very early twentieth century it also has personnel documents for the Regular Army, the Navy, the Marines, and the Coast Guard. In addition, the Archives has records relating to those who served in the Confederate Army or Navy and records relating to claims filed for veterans' pensions through 1916.

The military service records of those who fought in wars and rebellions from 1775 to 1903 are conveniently organized into compiled records that include information about a soldier taken from such diverse sources as muster rolls, payrolls, returns, hospital registers, and prison records. Composite records from these documents were made with enough care so that you need not spend time searching for the originals. Compiled service records usually disclose a person's rank and unit, his date of entry into service, and the date and nature of his discharge or separation. They may also indicate the soldier's age, his place of birth, and his residence at enlistment time. Various indexes are available to make access to those records easy. Except for the Civil War, they are organized alphabetically within each war or rebellion. The Civil War indexes are organized by state and by units with no state designation, such as the U.S. Sharp Shooters and the U.S. Signal Corps.

Military records more recent than those maintained by the Archives are filed at the National Personnel Records Center in St. Louis, Missouri. Records of the last seventy-five years are closed to public inspection. The government will supply only a limited amount of information from these confidential records to members of the immediate family, with the written consent of the serviceman if he is still alive.

The information in military records varies a great deal. Most are primarily useful for documenting military service and gleaning a few basic facts about the soldier. But they may yield unexpected details of family history. Civil War draft records are rich sources of information on all those eligible for military service, including volunteers. From these records you can usually learn an ancestor's place of residence, his age as of July 1, 1863, his occupation, his marital status, his state, territory, or country of birth, and if he had volunteered, his military organization. You may also find a personal description, an exact place of birth, and a designation of whether he was accepted or rejected for military duty. To locate these records you need to know the person's name and the congressional district in which he lived in 1863. Draft registration forms from World War I include such data as a man's address, date of birth, race, citizenship, occupation; the name and address of an employer; and the name and location of his nearest relative. For those registrants who actually were subject to the draft, questionnaires include additional information. You can obtain an ancestor's World War I draft records from the Federal Archives and Records Center, GSA, East Point, Georgia 30344. You will need sufficient knowledge of his residence to identify his selective service board.

Records of service in regular forces are kept separately for enlisted men and officers. These records are organized into a bewildering network of separate categories that demand dozens of pages of description in Linder and Walker's *Guide to Genealogical Records.* The most detailed records available for enlisted men will reveal a man's name, age, occupation, personal description, place of birth, date and place of enlistment, military unit, and the date and nature of his separation from the service. Officers' records may also supply additional information about the individual's service record.

Perhaps most useful to family historians are records of claims for military pensions. In several large rooms at the National Archives, rows of brown boxes are filled with hundreds of thousands of pension and payment records for veterans, widows, and other heirs. They relate to service in the Army, Navy, and Marines performed from 1775 to

1916. The contents of a pension file will vary according to the time of service and the facts of an individual case. Particularly for the period after 1860, you can routinely expect to find a veteran's claim containing information about his military service, date and place of birth, and current residence. A widow's claim will likely include the date and place of marriage, the maiden name of the wife, information about military service, the date and place of the veteran's death, and the names of dependent children. Researchers are often startled by what else can be found in the pension files. To prove matrimony, women sent copies of their original marriage licenses or even pictures of themselves and the veteran. Some claimants mailed in war citations and medals to prove that an individual had indeed served in the military. Medical records often accompanying requests shed light on the veteran's health and the medical practice of the time. One pension record goes on for many pages, containing the detailed and intimate testimony of two women who both claim to be the wife of a deceased veteran. Pension records are indexed according to the period of a veteran's service.

Provided with sufficient information, the National Archives staff will search for the military record of an ancestor and will send you copies of documents. According to Archives policy, you will usually need to supply them with the full name of the serviceman, the war in which he served, the state from which he entered service, and any other identifying information. The Archives will send you copies of GSA Form 6751, Order for Copies—Veterans Records, which details the procedures for making requests. Don't assume, however, that research by the Archives staff will turn up records for every ancestor who served in the military or applied for a pension. Some records are misfiled. Others (particularly those for the Revolutionary War) have been lost or destroyed, and problems regarding names and identification may foil your search. If possible, visit the National Archives in person.

FEDERAL LAND RECORDS

In the National Archives the federal government maintains records of original entry for title to land in the public-land states (all states of the Union except the original thirteen states, Kentucky, Maine, Vermont, West Virginia, Tennessee, Texas, and Hawaii, which are state-land states). These records include credit and cash sales of land, claims for land allegedly granted before the United States acquired sovereignty, grants of land in return for military service or certain conditions of settlement, and grants of land under the Homestead Act of 1862. Records of land entries include only information about the land and the transaction, the purchaser's name, and the county of residence at the time of the sale. The other types of records usually yield more personal data; of these, documents related to homesteading are likely to be most familiar to family historians.

During the era of Abraham Lincoln, not only did the Republican party struggle against slavery and secession, but it also sought to advance the development of American business and promote settlement in Western lands. Under provisions of the Homestead Act, passed in the second year of Lincoln's first term, citizens could acquire 160 acres of public land provided they agreed to cultivate and build a house on the land, and to reside there for five years. A complete homestead file generally will describe the tract of land, the house, the nature of the crops, and the number of acres being cultivated. It will also indicate the claimant's name, post office address, the number of family members and their relationship to the claimant, and proof of citizenship. For a naturalized citizen or one who intended to become naturalized, the papers will also include the place of his birth, and the date and port of his arrival.

Linder and Walker's *Guide to Genealogical Records*

warns that searching for federal land records can be an arduous task. For transactions after June 30, 1908, the Bureau of Land Management in Washington, D.C., has name indexes with numbers of the corresponding land-entry files. Scattered name indexes are available for some earlier transactions in some states, but generally you will need to know at least the approximate date of the transaction and the approximate location of the land. Even with this information, a search can still be difficult, expensive, and time consuming.

In studying federal land records, you would do well to check records of neighboring claims. Relatives or other groups of people may have claimed land next to one another. One researcher knew that an ancestor had acquired public land in a certain Illinois county, yet he could find no trace of his relative in the appropriate land records. After examining other claims in the vicinity he learned that his ancestor had migrated west as a member of a large religious sect. The ownership of the land was in the names of the church leaders. Examination of records pertaining to these leaders disclosed the size of the ancestor's family and the exact location of his land.

OTHER FEDERAL RECORDS

Other records of the federal government, far too numerous to discuss, may tell you something about an ancestor. The National Archives has records of claims brought before Congress, of merchant seamen, of passport applications, of residents in the District of Columbia. Regional Branch Archives have useful court records. The New York City Branch also has records for Puerto Rico. The Immigration and Naturalization Service, 425 I Street N.W., Washington, D.C. 20536, has records for people naturalized after September 26, 1906 (ask for Form G-641, which explains how to get nonconfidential information from these records). The National Personnel Records Center,

111 Winnebago Street, St. Louis, Missouri 63118, has most personnel records for federal employees. These records are closed for seventy-five years.

RECORDS OF PRIVATE ORGANIZATIONS

In your search for family history don't ignore the records of churches, business firms, and fraternal orders. However, these documents are generally not indexed or available from central repositories. Your access to these records will depend greatly upon prior knowledge of an ancestor's activities.

CHURCH RECORDS

"God is dead," proclaimed the German philosopher Nietzsche late in the nineteenth century. But few Americans seemed to hear him. Religion has flourished in twentieth-century America; despite a brief setback during the turbulent 1960's, church membership and participation in church organizations has steadily increased. Indeed, the church has always been a center of American society, functioning not only as a place of worship but also as a focal point of political and social life.

Churches, from the smallest Baptist congregation to the largest Catholic diocese, have all maintained records in one form or another. Because each religious institution is different, the content and value of these records will vary a great deal. Most churches record baptisms, christenings, marriages, and burials, creating documents that serve the same purpose as vital records of state and local governments and can be especially useful when government records do not exist. Church records may also contain information about family relationships, occupations, and status within the community. Remember, too, that baptisms were not restricted to children. An ancestor who at thirty years of age converted to a new sect may appear in the church's baptismal certificates.

Church records include valuable membership rolls and records of disciplinary activities. In addition to members' names, these lists may record the names and ages of family members, the dates of membership, the names and locations of previous churches, and the name and location of any church to which the ancestor may have transferred. These records may help you trace the movements of your ancestors, one of the most difficult tasks for the family historian. Records of disciplinary proceedings may supply fascinating biographical details on such matters as adultery, blasphemy, gambling, church attendance, and financial contributions.

Be sure to look at the business and financial proceedings of a church. These records may contain information about the donations of members, ministers' salaries, charitable ventures, and the cost and upkeep of church property. They may also describe the membership and activities of such church organizations as the membership committee, the hospitality committee, and the board of deacons. Does your ancestor emerge as a pillar of the church? Matters arising within a church may also reflect events in the economic and political life of the community. Political rivalries have led many churches to split into hostile warring factions.

As valuable as church records can be, they still pose formidable problems for the researcher. Thousands of religious organizations in America have appeared and have also disappeared. Even if you can determine your ancestor's religious affiliation, you must still find out where church records are located. Even then, you might find that the records you want are missing, destroyed, illegible, or impossible to interpret. During the 1930's, for example, many people turned to the teachings of the black mystic who called himself Father Divine. Thousands of people who may have been Baptists or Catholics left their churches to follow Divine's program of peace, love, and neighborhood service. Traditional records would offer only an incomplete and misleading picture of the religious life of any ancestor who followed Father Divine. The logical step would seem to be to examine the records of the "Divine Church." The true followers of this black prophet, however, do not allow nonmembers to rummage through the church's records. Even if you could study the records, you would probably find no trace of your ancestor, since participants in this religion replaced their Christian names with such names as "True Light," "Heavenly Trust," and "Flower of Peace."

Several valuable guides can point your way to the existence and location of church records, particularly for states east of the Mississippi River. Two of the best are E. Kay Kirkham's *A Survey of American Church Records* (east of the Mississippi River) and the October 1961 issue of the *American Archivist.* In looking through guides to church records be alert to the centralization of records by major churches, to the collection and copying of records by libraries and historical societies, and to the publication of early church records. If possible, visit your ancestor's local church and speak to elderly members and to pastors. Even if they do not remember your ancestor they may provide helpful background information. Records going back hundreds of years may be retained by local churches, sometimes neatly typed by workers of the WPA.

RECORDS OF SOCIAL AND FRATERNAL ORGANIZATIONS

America, Alexis de Tocqueville told the world in 1835, is a nation of joiners, a land of voluntary societies. Thousands of social and fraternal groups have indeed sprouted on American soil, offering people the excitement of secret rituals, the satisfaction of companionship, the security of belonging to a community, release from a boring job, or escape from a tense situation at home. Most of these organizations have maintained membership rolls that contain such information as a member's name, his date and place of birth, his occupation, the names of his children, spouses, and parents, his religious, social, and political affiliations, his educational and military history, his personal description, and perhaps even a photograph. Records of social and fraternal orders may also include the names and addresses of friends and relatives who recommended the member or served as references.

The names of larger fraternal and social organizations are familiar to most Americans—the Elks, the Masons, the Sons of Italy, the Odd Fellows, the B'nai Brith, the Shriners, and of course, college fraternities and sororities. If, for example, you know that an ancestor attended college, the odds are pretty good that he belonged to a fraternity. After consulting William Raimond Baird's *Manual of American College Fraternities* to learn what fraternities were active at that college during his stay, you can seek records of his possible membership from the secretaries of those organizations. If a fraternity no longer exists, you may be able to locate its records by contacting the National Inter-fraternity Conference. Your ancestors may have joined smaller organizations as well. Many Americans, for example, belonged to local burial societies (Oscar Handlin relates in *The Uprooted* that upon arrival in the New World, immigrants immediately arranged for their burial) that required proof of ethnic or religious heritage along with other information. Once you overcome the problems of determining an ancestor's social and fraternal affiliations and locating relevant records, you may find that officers of a society are reluctant to release their records. If possible, demonstrate your relationship to the member (and get his authorization if he is still living); show your sincerity of purpose and you may well gain access to the documents.

EDUCATIONAL RECORDS

Private education in America began in the early years of colonial settlement. Anxious to provide training for the ministry, Congregationalists (Puritans) in New England organized Harvard University in 1636. Competing religions later began their own colleges; in 1693 the Anglicans founded William and Mary, and in 1746 the Presbyterians opened Princeton University. Individuals and groups also began private elementary and secondary schools throughout the colonies, offering in many areas the only available education for boys and girls. Often closely tied to religious groups, private schools and colleges have continued to flourish in the United States up to the present time. School and college records include applications for admission and financial aid (which may be laced with data about the applicant and his family), records of registration, matriculation, graduation, grades, and payment, and perhaps even letters of recommendation, reports of outside activities, and a sample of an ancestor's prose. Educational institutions also publish yearbooks, biographies, histories, and alumni bulletins which may contain information about an ancestor. If family sources do not reveal where an ancestor attended school, you can check institutions in the vicinity of his residence, using religion as a clue to the school he most likely would have attended. Of course, schools in America are frequently created and abandoned, so identification of an ancestor's institution is no guarantee of access to records. Only the most fortunate of researchers will find records of a defunct institution at a historical society, a sister institution, or the headquarters of the sponsoring religious order. Moreover, early records, particularly for elementary and secondary schools, often were not carefully maintained or have been lost, destroyed, or discarded. And in some cases, more recent records may be considered confidential by an institution. (To gain access to these records, use the same tactics recommended for gaining access to records of fraternal orders.) Despite these problems, digging in school records may reward you with much information.

BUSINESS AND LABOR RECORDS

For most of American history, people were self-employed as farmers and craftsmen, or they worked for others on farms and in small shops and businesses. Records of such employment were either never kept or have long since passed into oblivion. As the nation industrialized during the nineteenth century, enterprises steadily became larger and more complex, and grew more concerned with obtaining and maintaining records about their employees. If an ancestor worked for a major business firm that still exists in some form (many businesses have merged to form new outfits while retaining previous records), you might be able to write for a record of his employment. Although the contents of these records vary, the more modern the record, the more likely it is to have detailed information. Most employment files will at least provide the employee's name, address, age, previous job experience, and some general comments about him. If an ancestor was himself a businessman you might find an analysis of his financial standing in the records of Dun and Bradstreet; if he was a doctor or lawyer, professional associations may possess details of his biography. Insurance companies, banks, and credit unions may also have information about his financial activities. During the twentieth century, credit bureaus have maintained extensive files on individuals with detailed (although often erroneous) information about their lives. With a little tact and a little money you may be able to get these credit reports.

RECORDS OF HEREDITARY SOCIETIES

Membership in some societies is conditional upon descent from an ancestor identified with a certain event, period, or locale. The National Society of the Daughters of the American Revolution is the most famous of the hereditary societies. Male and female descendants of wars from the American Revolution to the Spanish-American War of 1898 have formed similar societies. Norman Wright's *Building an American Pedigree* (pp. 401–402) and the D.A.R.'s pamphlet "Is That Lineage Right?" both offer partial lists of hereditary societies. The Daughters of the American Revolution have published lineage books of its members and at its library in Washington, D.C., maintains unpublished lineage records that are open for inspection if the member has died, resigned, or been dropped from the society or if the member has given written authorization to a researcher. The D.A.R. also has an index of Revolutionary patriots "on whose service members have entered" the society. Similarly, other hereditary societies keep useful records of their members' ancestries.

ADDITIONAL PRIVATE RECORDS

Many other private records might be worth investigating. Morticians and cemetery officials keep records that may date before 1900 and include considerable personal data on the deceased. Reports of hospitals, orphanages, and welfare agencies, if open for examination, may supply information about an ill, orphaned, or destitute ancestor. For a variety of reasons, private organizations occasionally took valuable local surveys and censuses. At various times during the 1830's and 1840's, for example, abolition societies in Philadelphia conducted a census of the black community, offering information that is available from no other source. Organizations, individuals, and families have manuscript collections stored in major libraries and historical societies which include such items as financial records, letters, and scrapbooks.

PRINTED SOURCES

Some students of family history are so eager to find original records of their heritage that they ignore what can be learned from already printed and published sources. In addition to printed copies of primary documents like wills and deeds, printed sources include general and local history, newspapers and directories, compiled genealogies, and articles in genealogical magazines. Don't forget that publication is no guarantee of truth. Any work is only as reliable as the author, his methods, and his evidence. Regard what you read with skepticism and try if possible to seek verification before accepting an author's claims to the truth.

AMERICAN HISTORY

Familiarity with American history is a substantial asset for a family historian. The lives of ancestors and their families cannot be separated from the events of their times. Unless you knew something about the Revolutionary War, information relating to the service of a patriot ancestor would have very little meaning for you. Unless you knew that in much of the nation an agricultural depression of the 1920's preceded the general depression of the 1930's, you might badly misinterpret the experiences of a farmer-grandfather. Knowledge of history also provides the fun and excitement of comparing the experiences of your own ancestors with the group experiences described by historians. Beginners in American history should read through a respected text like *The National Experience* by John Morton Blum et al., or John A. Garraty's *The American Nation.* Textbooks usually include bibliographies that lead you to more specialized literature. The *Harvard Guide to American History,* edited by Frank Freidel, is a definitive reference for work published through 1970. For an introduction to more recent literature you can consult the articles and book reviews in the *Journal of American History*, available at most large libraries.

By dipping into the history of the family, you gain a firmer grasp of the themes and topics that can be pursued in your own project. Unfortunately, much of the new family history is not readily accessible to most readers. Often filled with statistics and the jargon of social science, family history is written primarily for those with special training and is published as scholarly articles. We still await a second generation of work that will present family history to a general audience. *The American Family in Social-Historical Perspective* (revised edition), edited by Michael Gordon, is a useful collection of essays. The truly ambitious reader should go to a university or a major public library and consult recent issues of such scholarly journals as the *Journal of Social History*, the *Journal of Interdisciplinary History*, the *Journal of Marriage and the Family*, and the *Journal of Family History*.

LOCAL HISTORIES

Works written about neighborhoods, towns, counties, and even states may actually mention an ancestor of yours or at least describe the community in which he lived and events that may have touched his life. Be aware, however, that such histories are often prepared by patriots eager to celebrate the heritage of their locality. Try to check any factual material extracted from local histories, and be wary of any historical interpretations put forth by the writer. Most local histories, however, are narratives of events and descriptions of individuals, local landmarks, and organizations that shun analysis and interpretation. Local histories are often found in local libraries and historical societies; the Library of Congress in Washington, D.C., also has a superb collection of these works.

NEWSPAPERS AND DIRECTORIES

Newspapers are a valuable and accessible source for the family historian. Don't restrict your research to the major metropolitan dailies, but try to examine local papers such as the *Belleville Times* or the *Tombstone Epitaph.* Stories about local events may include information about your ancestors, as might notices of births, engagements, and marriages, and reports of legal proceedings. Obituaries, a studied source for family history, usually contain the deceased person's name, age, occupation, family relationships, residence, and at times, the cause of his death. They may also include biographical information about someone notable in the locality. Beyond offering information about forebears, local newspapers evoke the atmosphere of life in a community. They report the ebb and flow of community events, indicate social standing within the community, reveal what people do for recreation, and disclose how they choose their political leaders. They contain advertisements that offer glimpses of local styles; tastes and customs; medical practices; and the availability of goods, services, and transportation. Newspapers report marriages, engagements, social events, ship arrivals, and weather reports. The historian who pages through newspapers may also find such tidbits as recipes, cartoons, sermons, political speeches, bankruptcy notices, and advice to individuals.

Daily, weekly, and bimonthly newspapers have been published for counties, towns, cities, and even neighborhoods. They have catered to entire communities or served such specialized audiences as nationality and religious groups. You may find copies of old papers in newspaper morgues, public libraries, historical societies, state libraries, and universities.*

*Clarence Saunders Brigham, *History and Bibliography of American Newspapers, 1690-1820* (reprinted by Greenwood Press in Westport,

Directories of individuals have been published for cities and towns, for those in certain businesses and professions, for telephone subscribers. These directories may tell you an individual's occupation and his political affiliations. Directories often include advertisements, maps, descriptions of business enterprises, and information about local governments. Notable ancestors might also be listed in *Who's Who in America* (or in one of its specialized volumes like *Who's Who in the East*) or might appear in one of the many published biographical dictionaries.

COMPILED GENEALOGIES AND GENEALOGICAL MAGAZINES

While very few people have published histories on the inner workings of family life, many have published genealogies that set forth their family tree. Genealogists have also published articles on particular families (as well as original source material) in genealogical magazines. Imagine how exciting it could be to find a compiled genealogy for your own family that might portray relationships you never would have discovered or trace family lines through several centuries of history. One family-history student found a compiled genealogy that traced a branch of his father's family to a ninth-century king of Brittany. But don't assume that the study of a compiled genealogy is an easy shortcut to research. Many amateur genealogists weren't familiar with rigorous standards of research and were eager to find notable ancestors. Thus published genealogies have been found to contain many errors of fact (although standards have improved in recent years). "Many works," according to Milton Rubincam, past president of the National Genealogical Society and the

---

Connecticut, 1976), and Winifred Gregory, ed., *American Newspapers 1821-1936—A Union List of Files Available in the United States and Canada* (New York: H. W. Wilson, 1937) are useful guides for locating extant newspapers.

American Society of Genealogists, "are not worth the paper on which they are printed. They are carelessly done, their compilers being untrained and inexperienced in methods of genealogical research and presentation." Among several examples of careless work, he cites one genealogy in which a claimed descent from a governor of Connecticut would have been possible only if the governor's wife had been "about twenty-one years old when her alleged *grandson* was born!" When using compiled genealogies, consider the reliability of the compiler and the adequacy of the evidence, if any, cited in support of the claims that are made. You can safely use them for formulating hypotheses about your family history which can then be tested with other, more reliable evidence.

Compiled genealogies and magazine articles may be located in local libraries and historical and genealogical libraries. The Library of Congress has an outstanding collection of published genealogies, as does the D.A.R., the Newberry Library in Chicago, and the Library of the Genealogical Society of the Latter-Day Saints in Salt Lake City, Utah. There is no single master index that will tell you if a book or article on a family line has been published and where it is located. But there are many partial indexes, arranged by surname, which can be of great assistance to the researcher. For a discussion of the indexes available through 1972, see Wright, *Building an American Pedigree* (pp. 86–115).

THE GENEALOGICAL SOCIETY OF THE LATTER-DAY SAINTS

The D.A.R. was once considered the fount of American genealogy, but no longer. The Genealogical Society of the Church of Jesus Christ of Latter-Day Saints is now the nation's leading promoter of genealogy and the most bountiful source of research material. The unsurpassed and steadily expanding collection of the Genealogical Society includes more than 150,000 books and more than 1,200,000 rolls of microfilmed records (faultlessly preserved deep in the Wasach Mountains near Salt Lake City). Recorded on microfilm are such documents as wills, deeds, land grants, marriage records, cemetery inscriptions, and passenger arrival lists. The records range over hundreds of years and contain items from nations all over the world. The genealogical storehouse of the Latter-Day Saints is open to the public; you need not be a member of the church.

The Mormons expend so much time, energy, and money on genealogy because they believe that they can posthumously bring ancestors into the church. A deceased ancestor identified by a church member can still be baptized at a formal ceremony held at one of the Mormon temples. If the ancestor accepts this initiation in the hereafter he will be united with other baptized members of his family.

The Genealogical Society can aid your family history research first by offering you access to its books and original records. The society's main library is located in Salt Lake City, Utah (50 East North Temple St., Salt Lake City, Utah 84150), but it has over two hundred branches located all over the country. Branch libraries have microfilm copies of the main library's card catalogue and can borrow copies of books and microfilms to be consulted on the premises. You should visit rather than write to a branch library, since they generally are not equipped to handle mail inquiries. The society also maintains, in its Salt Lake City library, indexes of family group records submitted by members of the church as well as indexes of particular names mentioned in these documents. There might, for example, be a family group record for a line of the Braithwaite family, or Hamilton Braithwaite might be mentioned in one or more group records. Records kept by the church include the ancestors of many non-Mormons as well as members of the Latter-Day Saints. If you are fortunate, the search might yield several generations of ancestors. For a moderate fee, staff members will research these indexes of more than fifty million names, looking for individuals from one branch of your family tree. Even if the staff can find no trace of family members, they will still supply you with suggestions for further research and a list of genealogists working in your area of interest. But don't assume that information on family members arising from such a search is necessarily correct. As with other secondary records you should, if possible, try to verify the claims that are made. The staff of the Genealogical Society, however, won't perform research in original records.

SOCIETIES AND LIBRARIES IN WASHINGTON, D.C.

Despite the strides made by the Latter-Day Saints, the nation's capital still is the mecca of genealogy due to the National Archives and Records Service, the main repository of federal records, the National Genealogical Society, the National Society of the Daughters of the American Revolution, and the Library of Congress.

The National Genealogical Society was established in 1903 to promote interest and scholarly research nationwide in genealogy. Its library, located at 1921 Sunderland Place N.W., Washington, D.C. 20036, is open to the public for a fee of $1.00 per visit and includes both published and unpublished material in genealogy, local history, and heraldry. Membership in the society costs $20.00 per year and includes free use of the library, the *National Genealogical Society Quarterly* and *Newsletter,* access to the "members ancestors charts" of other members, opportunities to make brief genealogical inquiries through the mails, and invitations to society meetings. For a one-time enrollment fee of $5.00 and a small charge for each request, members can also borrow by mail most of the published works in the society's library. This can be a very important service for people without access to a good genealogical library. The society will not research your family tree, but instead suggests that you request lists of qualified genealogists from the Board for Certification of Genealogists, 1307 New Hampshire Avenue N.W., Washington, D.C. 20036.

If research space at the relatively small library of the National Genealogical Society is at a premium, the library of the National Society of the Daughters of the American Revolution across town at 1776 D Street, N.W., Washington, D.C. 20006 is bright and airy with plenty of space. The library has an excellent genealogical collection, especially for colonial America. In addition to published works, the library has copies of local records made by members of chapters throughout the country. It also has abstracts of Revolutionary War pensions, federal census schedules from 1850 to 1880, various mortality schedules, member's genealogies, and its index of patriots. Despite its reputation for exclusivity, the D.A.R. Library is open to the public (for a fee of $1.00) except during the month of April. The D.A.R. doesn't provide research services, but will photocopy and mail specifically identified material to researchers for a small fee.

The Library of Congress also maintains an extensive collection of genealogical material, available through its Local History and Genealogy Room. Most notable are the library's 30,000 published family histories (arranged and indexed by surname) and its 90,000 works on local history. The library has a catalogue of surnames and individuals referred to in selected works of local history. For a complete list of the library's genealogical holdings, see the *Guide to Genealogical Holdings at the Library of Congress* and the *Guide to Local History at the Library of Congress,* available at any major library. For a per-page fee along with mailing and packing charges, the library will photocopy and mail specifically cited pages from a book or a record listed in the guide to the holdings of the Library of Congress. Upon request, the General Reference and Bibliography Division will distribute free of charge two useful bibliographies: "Guides to Genealogical Research: A Selected List" and "Surnames: A Selected List of References."

RESEARCH IN RECORDS OF FOREIGN NATIONS

Unlike partisan politics, family history does not stop at the water's edge. You may wish to pursue the search for your heritage into the sources available in Europe, Africa, Asia, or Latin America. You may even want to visit any ancestral homeland, bridging for yourself the gap between your life in America today and the lives of ancestors from another land. Along with details of your history you might discover relatives still living in places occupied by your ancestors more than a thousand years ago. Whether your search leads you to Chad in Africa or Geneva in Switzerland, searching for your history abroad can be a difficult but immensely rewarding effort.

Research in foreign nations must begin in the United States. Before traveling abroad, amass as much information as possible about the ancestors you hope to trace. The more information you collect, the more successful your search for records will be. Before turning to foreign repositories, also check the microfilm holdings of the Genealogical Society of the Latter-Day Saints. You may find that they already possess some foreign records that include mention of your ancestors. For research in most countries you should at least know the complete name of your ancestor and any nicknames he may have used; the name of the country of origin as well as the local region, county, or parish; the approximate date of migration to America. Any additional information, such as the names of contemporary relatives or family members, will also be helpful.

Several sources offer easily accessible information on what records are available in foreign lands and how you can go about requesting them. In *The Genealogist's Encyclopedia*, Leslie G. Pine lists records and repositories for most European countries as well as for nations on other continents. In *Finding Our Fathers*, Dan Rottenberg discusses sources abroad for Jewish family records, and in *Black Genealogy*, Charles L. Blockson and Ron Fry do the same for records of black families. *Genealogical Research Methods and Sources,* volumes I and II (Milton Rubincam, ed.), traces migration from Europe to America and analyzes what is available in various nations of Europe. The Genealogical Society of the Latter-Day Saints and officials of foreign embassies can tell you where to write for foreign records and can alert you to special problems of research in a particular nation. Several foreign nations including Canada, Great Britain, Norway, Sweden, and the Netherlands have published guides to genealogical research in their nations. The Library of Congress owns these guides and lists them in its guide to genealogical research.

You can follow several strategies for doing research in foreign nations. You can write directly to the agencies responsible. Be sure to enclose international postal reply coupons in any request for information and to expect a fee for searching and copying documents. You can ask friends and relatives living or traveling abroad to perform a research task for you, provided that you give them sufficient guidance. You can also hire professional help overseas, often by contacting an historical or genealogical society in the country and region of interest. Of course, there is no substitute for actually journeying to another country and searching for your own roots.

Try to become familiar with the location and the history of your ancestral homelands. Your ancestor, for example, may have immigrated from Rumania, but her home province may now be part of the Soviet Union. Looking through history books and old maps can save you hours of blind research. Maps of eighteenth- and nineteenth-century European countries are available for a fee, from Karta

Europe, 7212 44th St. N.W., Seattle, Washington 98117. Karta Europe will even send you maps of an ancestor's locality if you can tell them the name of an ancestor's town (include variant spellings); the name of the province that the town was in, and any descriptive information about the town and its immediate environment (for example, was the town in the mountains or in a valley?).

For some Americans, research abroad means discovery of the family's coat of arms. Indeed, upon payment of a fee, commercial outfits will send you a facsimile and description of the coat of arms allegedly belonging to your family. If authentic at all, these mail-order certificates indicate only that these arms belonged to someone with your family name, but not necessarily to an ancestor of yours. Coats of arms generally were granted to or assumed by particular individuals and thereafter conveyed by certain rules of descent. Research in this realm (termed "heraldry") can become complicated and often demands special expertise. For a brief introduction to heraldry that tells how you can legitimately acquire a coat of arms, consult the chapter by J. Charles Thompson in the American Genealogical Research Institute's *How to Trace Your Family Tree.*

Some of the genealogy books appearing in the wake of Alex Haley's *Roots* deceptively suggest the ease of tracing your ancestors to a homeland abroad. Research in records outside the home can be difficult and the search for records abroad only compounds these difficulties. But fruitful research in foreign records can be done. Just be sure to plan your work with special care and to exhaust resources in the United States first.

SPECIAL SOURCES OF RECORDS

Minority groups in this country have faced historical circumstances that make family-history research especially difficult. Until recently historians have neglected the past of America's minority peoples and have been negligent in keeping, preserving, and indexing minority-group records. By way of illustration, consider the specific examples of blacks and Native Americans.

BLACKS

The publication of *Roots* shattered the myth that black family history couldn't be done, and thousands of blacks began searching for a heritage that once seemed beyond reach. At the same time there has been a proliferation of guides on how to do black genealogy. Blockson and Fry's *Black Genealogy* is a readable work that contains a useful directory of research sources both in the United States and abroad. It also lists black newspapers and white newspapers that published slave advertisements.

Records of blacks before the Civil War are sketchy and difficult to use. There are thousands of records of slave sales, slave importation, and punishment meted out to slaves. But these documents are not of much use unless you have an idea of what plantation your ancestor lived on and what he was called by the master. (Most slaves had no last names, greatly complicating problems of research.) Although records relating to free blacks are also scattered, these families can be traced in the federal census, in tax records, and in court documents. Many jurisdictions also kept tallies of the numbers and locations of free blacks. Black newspapers, white newspapers with mentions of slave sales and runaways, records of black churches, military records, minutes and proceedings of abolitionist societies, and records of the Freedman's Bureau may also be of assistance.

INDIANS

American Indians face a difficult task in tracing their family history through outside sources of information. Throughout American history there has been a gulf between Indian culture and that of the European. Although the white man's superior technology eventually led to the military domination of the Indian, government policy regarding the Indian has wavered erratically. At times the government wanted to keep the Indian on the reservation living in much the same way as his forefathers. But at other times the government has attempted to destroy tribal culture and assimilate the Indian to the white man's world.

Most surviving Indian records originated in these relationships between the government and the Native American. The National Archives has federal records that pertain to Indians arranged by tribe, so that information on an ancestor's tribal affiliation is a prerequisite for research. Included in these records are lists of Eastern Indians, mainly members of the five "civilized" tribes whom the government moved west along the "trail of tears." These lists enumerate family names, ages, sex, and relationships of individuals living in households. They also list the property owned by the Indian and the dates of departure from the East and arrival in the West. The Archives' collection also includes annuity payrolls that record welfarelike payments to Indians, and territorial and federal censuses of the Indian population. In addition, the Archives has the files of the Carlisle Indian School, attended by many Indians of the Midwest and the East. The Genealogical Society of the Latter-Day Saints has collections of records relating to Indians, and the Indian Archives Division of the Oklahoma Historical Society has a book listing members of the five civilized tribes by age, sex, degree of Indian blood, and census-card number. Many tribal councils maintain records dating from the 1920's, and scattered records can be found in localities throughout the nation.

Indian records must be interpreted with care. You should try to become familiar with the history of your tribe, paying special attention to patterns of naming and systems of kinship. The records concerning Indians maintained by white men were often carelessly kept and may have reflected misunderstandings of Indian culture.

The study of sources outside the home requires more specialized knowledge than any other phase of family-history research. Even after learning what sources exist and where they are located, you must still be prepared to cope with missing records, obsolete forms of handwriting, restricted access to documents, and changes in names, boundaries, calendars, and currencies. Fortunately, much help is available from reference works, librarians, archivists, genealogists, and historians. With patience and diligence you can begin a fruitful search for documents that can transport you through several hundred years of family history.

Chapter 7

PLANNING AND COMPLETING YOUR RESEARCH

IN THE BOOKS OF HISTORIANS, wrote Thomas Carlyle, "lies the *soul* of the whole Past Time; the articulate audible voice of the Past, when the body and material substance of it has altogether vanished like a dream." Your work in family history is the audible voice of your personal past, that special part of history whose soul is within your care. Without nourishment, the soul of your past would disappear as surely as any material body. In preserving your family's history you also help save a portion of our common heritage. As ordinary people become the protagonists of a new historical script, personal family histories become valuable source materials, capturing details of life that often elude the grasp of professionals. Many scholars now look forward to the time when they can use the works produced by today's family historians.

There is really no limit to the scope of your efforts to recover the family's past. Research continually creates a new horizon that invites you to further inquiry. To complete the study of one ancestor is to kindle curiosity about the life of another. Once you know which questions to ask, sources to explore, and methods to follow, you will have a strong foundation for studying family history. Your labors will be worthwhile if they help to preserve the voice of but a single ancestor.

For many of us, an interest in family history begins without planning or premeditation. Sudden inspiration, for example, brought Alex Haley to investigate mysteries locked within family stories told to him more than thirty years before. As a child, he had heard his grandmother speak of the family's "farthest-back person," an African who kept escaping from his plantation until slave catchers finally hacked off one of his feet. This African, she said, had insisted on calling himself "Kin-tay" and had fathered a daughter called "Kizzie." He would point out things to his daughter, repeating their names in his native tongue: a guitar he called "ko," the river, "Kamby Bolongo." Since the awakening of his interest in family history, Haley wrote that he had "traveled half a million miles . . . searching, sifting, checking, crosschecking, finding out more and more . . ."

GUIDANCE FOR RESEARCH

Few people have the time and resources to produce their own *Roots,* but no matter what the goal, duration, or intensity of your research, it will benefit from careful planning. Otherwise research can become an aimless quest for information that yields a warehouse of notes but little understanding of family history. So first develop a list of carefully thought out questions that should indicate the themes you intend to explore and perhaps set forth the time period you anticipate covering and the branches of the family you plan to include (see Chapter 2 for a discussion of possible themes).

Like a tour map, questions should lead you to interesting places and keep you moving toward your final destination. But questions should not bind you inflexibly to an itinerary planned in advance. As you proceed, ask new questions and modify or even discard those you had earlier planned to consider. You should be ready to follow leads suggested by your evidence or to pursue fresh inspiration. During the course of your project, pause frequently to think about what you have already accomplished and what you still plan to do.

BIBLIOGRAPHY

Your next step is to compile a list of the sources you anticipate using. Your bibliography should be comprehensive, including people to be interviewed; family papers, objects, and photographs; and documents found outside the home. Identify each entry as completely as possible, including the author, title, publisher, and place of publication for each printed source. You might also mention how you became aware of a source and indicate what you might learn from it and where it can be found. Try to leave space on all bibliographic entries to record when and where you actually looked at source material.

For easy reference, divide your bibliography into distinct categories. For example:

1. Oral-history interviews
2. Family documents
3. Material objects
4. Family photographs and movies
5. State and local records
6. Federal records
7. Records of foreign nations
8. Records of private organizations
9. Published sources

Within each of these categories you should create further subdivisions, classifying, for example, compiled genealogies, directories, local histories, general histories, newspapers, magazines, and maps as subdivisions of published sources. Within each subdivision, you could list material alphabetically or according to common locations.

Your initial bibliography is a working tool, not a finished product. As your inquiry proceeds, you will continually be adding new items. Your research might unexpectedly reveal that an ancestor had served as a volunteer in the Mexican War of 1848, leading to the addition of his military records to the sources you expect to examine.

TAKING AND ARRANGING NOTES

Before seeking the sources catalogued in your bibliography, first decide how to record and arrange your findings. Generally research notes should be written on file cards, which can be arranged and rearranged, rather than on the pages of notebooks. Instead of standard index cards, you might want to use keysort cards, which have small holes punched around their borders. Each separately numbered hole can represent a different category in a filing system. If the notes on a card fall into a particular category, the hole corresponding to that category is broken to the edge of the card. You can quickly isolate all entries within a category by passing a metal rod through the appropriate hole in a stack of keysort cards. All cards with holes broken to the edge will fall out, whereas all others will remain strung out along the rod. You don't have to keep your keysort cards in any particular order, since you can always use the metal rod to select cards from any category. The keysort system enables you to cross-reference note cards according to several different classification schemes. A 4-inch-by-6-inch card will probably have about eighty holes, each of which can stand for a category within a system of classification.

To identify individual file cards, transcribe the full bibliographic citation, including page number, on the top of the card. Or keep a master list of references, numbering each source and recording the appropriate number on each card. You can use your bibliography as the master list, thus ensuring correspondence between citations on the bibliography and those on your notes. Whatever system you choose, be sure that all your notes are clearly identified. You don't want to encounter crucial pieces of information without being able to determine their origins.

Research notes can assume several different forms. Sometimes you will want only to summarize the content of a source, especially when using it primarily for background information. Be sure that your summaries are sufficiently clear to be comprehensible at a later date; notes that are too condensed or cryptic may force a needless reexamination of sources. Rather than summarizing material, you may sometimes want to paraphrase a few key passages or take down phrases, sentences, names, or statistics. You might, for instance, want to transcribe the names and ages of family members from a census report. Your objective would be to record the data accurately, but not necessarily to duplicate the exact form of the census document. Indeed, if you were copying names and ages for a large number of families, you could devise your own format for recording this data.

At times, however, you will want to duplicate an entire document or a substantial portion of it. Exact duplication is important when you expect to quote from a source or when the interpretation of evidence may depend upon its precise wording or format. Whenever you copy a quotation verbatim, be sure to identify it as such and to verify its accuracy. Rather than hand-copying long passages or tracing the form of a record, consider using a copying machine to reproduce the information you want and then jot down on a file card a brief description of the material copied. The use of copying facilities is especially recommended when you lack the time or energy to take detailed notes.

The abstracting of a document is a compromise between paraphrasing and exact duplication. An abstract records key phrases and sentences exactly as they appear in a document, indicating omissions with an ellipsis, the standard three-period sign. This technique is most appropriate for documents like wills and deeds that have a common form and a great deal of material that is not relevant to a family historian's interests. In abstracting a land sale document, for example, you would record the names of the buyer and seller as well as other personal data such as occupation and marital status. Your abstract would include the purchase price of the land, the conditions of purchase, the description and location of the land, and the date and place of the transaction. But the abstract would omit all the standard legal declarations routinely recorded for land transactions. Before abstracting any document, however, be sure you know what is standard and can be excluded.

A few mechanical rules are helpful in taking notes. Try to leave some space on your cards for your own comments, which should be clearly labeled and not confused with notes taken from the source. Try to take down only one note on each card. File cards crammed with different notes will be impossible to sort into separate categories. If you find yourself copying a quotation that extends to more than one card, consider duplicating the entire page or stapling several cards together. To avoid transcribing useless material, keep in mind the questions that you are trying to answer; when in doubt, take notes on the material rather than risking the loss of potentially valuable information. If continually perplexed about what to take down, you should consider revising your basic questions, perhaps narrowing their scope and sharpening their focus.

Be sure to devise an orderly system for arranging your note cards, your original documents, and your copies of documents. You can use whatever scheme best serves the purpose of your study, since no single system ideally suits every case. Rather than placing notes into single categories, historians usually divide the main categories of a filing system into several subdivisions. Within each subdivision, material often is arranged first by date and then alphabetically. A refined system of classification will not only facilitate access to material but will force you to think about how to organize your research.

In contrast to a bibliography, which generally is arranged according to the characteristics of sources, the arrangement of a research file usually follows the logic of the inquiry. A family historian accumulating information about individual ancestors might file notes first by an ancestor's name (surname, then first and middle name) and then by subject of interest (perhaps following the list of subjects on pp. 45–46). A family historian concerned primarily with tracing events over time might organize information first by date, then by name, and then by subject. An historian focusing on a particular theme might file notes first according to subdivisions of the theme and then by name and date. By using keysort cards, however, an historian could combine several of these schemes into a system of cross references.

The time and energy spent in planning family history will be repaid many times in the course of a project. Through careful preparation you avoid needless work and make the most of research you decide to do. For additional guidance on the planning of historical research you can consult Jacques Barzun and Henry F. Graff, *The Modern Researcher*, and Allan J. Lichtman and Valerie French, *Historians and the Living Past: The Theory and Practice of Historical Study*.

COMPILING SOURCES

Every family historian should preserve his collection of sources—records of interviews, letters, photographs, official documents, family heirlooms. These foundation stones of family history communicate a vivid and immediate sense of the past to whoever takes the time to study them. Familiarity with this material can also reveal new opportunities for research and save years of duplicate labor.

Some family historians have compiled volumes of such sources as permanent legacies for their families. Sort and file these items in acid-free folders to make your own sourcebook of family history. As you uncover fresh material, add, delete, or change the arrangement of papers. A collection of primary sources might portray the life of a single ancestor, running chronologically from birth to death. This memorial to an ancestor preserves the story of a life that would otherwise fade from memory. As another focus for a family-history sourcebook, you could choose a single episode or a specific theme from the family's past. Whatever the unifying thread of your collection, you can include identifying comments (who, for example, are the people mentioned in a letter?), background information (why did the family leave the farm for the city?), and historical analysis (what explains a discrepancy found in two different letters?).

You can add evidence to a book of family records that sets the family's experience in its proper historical context. Opposite the homestead petition of a great-grandfather, for instance, you might juxtapose the frontispiece of the original Homestead Act or a photograph of a typical homestead from your ancestor's region of settlement. The National Archives and Records Service and its regional branches can supply copies of historical documents and photographs. You can also seek assistance from state libraries and archives, and from state and local historical societies. The bibliography lists useful guides for finding historical pictures.

If you must select items for your sourcebook from a large corpus of material, look for sources that are rich in detail, that disclose a person's thoughts and feelings, that convey a vivid impression of what life was like in the past. Be sure to indicate the principles you followed in culling documents and to describe roughly what you have omitted. If you're swamped by an abundance of evidence, consider microfilming (if you can afford it) the entire collection, saving the microfilm as one form of record, and then selecting for your volume full-size copies made from the microfilm. Try to include complete documents rather than excerpts, and don't attempt to censor or in any way "correct" an original record. Your commentary can clarify vague references or indicate that contradictory evidence exists.

A family historian should pay attention to preserving the records of his or her own life. You are as integral to your family's history as an ancestor who died a hundred years ago. Why not help future historians of your family preserve your memory? Begin by surveying the papers in your possession and set up an orderly filing system. Add new items to your files as you acquire them; don't allow papers to pile up again and don't destroy what could be an important historical record. Keep copies of the letters you send and of other documents not retained in your possession. You can use the same system for both a working file and a personal archive, adding new categories and subdivisions as necessary. If you are married, work out a filing system with your wife or husband and your children. Also consider organizing and properly identifying your family photographs and heirlooms.

WRITTEN MANUSCRIPTS

Beyond the compilation of records, your lineage charts provide one kind of summary of the results of your research. They should be kept in proper form and checked for accuracy, clarity, and consistency. You can supplement these charts with lists of additional information gathered for ancestors; accounts of family stories, sayings, and traditions; reports of notable events and accomplishments. Be fair to your ancestors in these summaries of information.

Do not distort their lives by excluding what seems to be embarrassing or derogatory (while respecting, of course, any confidentiality agreements made with informants). Try to resist the temptation to revise the past according to the values of today.

You may decide to do more than collect records and summarize information. From your sources and your notes you can write an essay or even a book. Only the most ambitious of family historians will undertake a book-length study, but many of you will want to try composing an essay about some aspect of your family's past.

Rather than trying to cram your entire family history into a single essay, think about how you might develop a particular theme. By trying to say too much, we usually find ourselves saying very little of value. Successful essays usually focus on a fairly narrow, well-defined topic. Students, for example, have traced the migration patterns of colonial ancestors, have looked at privacy over several generations of family history, and have even studied the changing roles of animals in the life of the family. Whatever your subject, be sure to adapt your writing to your audience. Is your manuscript destined only for members of the immediate family, or do you seek wider circulation? Do you plan to try publishing your work in a genealogical or historical magazine? The choice of audience can affect every aspect of an essay from the points it stresses to the tone it strikes. You would probably adopt a more informal and chatty style for a work written for the family than for a class assignment or for publication. You might also entertain the family with anecdotes that would be of less interest to outside readers. Especially when writing for a general audience, don't assume that your readers will share your enthusiasm for every detail of your history.

SLIDE-TAPE SHOWS

Without draining your bank account or mastering difficult techniques, you can put together a slide-tape show that reproduces a slice of family history. Like a sourcebook or a written manuscript, a slide-tape program can follow the chronology of a life or treat a selected theme or episode. One successful show, created by Howell Green and presented at the National Archives and Records Service, focused on a grandfather's service as a British medic in the Boer War (fought in South Africa from 1899 to 1902).

A slide-tape presentation coordinates the projection of slides with the simultaneous playing of a tape. The changing of the slides is timed precisely to coincide with specific portions of the tape. The slides can reproduce old photographs and pictures, depict a home or an heirloom, display a document, or show a family member talking about the past. You can supplement your family's own collection by making slides of photographs, pictures, and documents available from historical collections. Lacking photographs from his grandfather, Howell Green was able to find pictures of preparations for service in the Boer War, of the voyage to South Africa, and of medical service in the war itself. The tape should include a narrative by the producer and carefully selected quotations, music, songs, sound effects, comments by family members, and information from historical sources. Green, for example, enriched his narrative with research into the history of his grandfather's outfit, the St. John's Ambulance Brigade. He quoted from contemporary newspapers and other historical documents as well as from the letters of his own ancestor. You could also organize a slide-tape program around the oral recollections of an ancestor. In this case, the ancestor's testimony can be the central narrative of the presentation.

FAMILY-HISTORY CLUBS AND ASSOCIATIONS

If you want to research and write family history, you need not labor alone. Not only can you join a genealogical or historical society, but you can also organize a family-history club in your local community. Although members of a family-history club might be studying their respective ancestries, they can still share one another's frustrations and accomplishments. They can exchange ideas about research techniques, information about access to sources, and experiences with repositories of records. Club members can read and comment on each other's writing, discuss published work in genealogy and family history, and even perform research tasks for one another. The club can be formally organized with dues, officers, and regular meetings. It could offer means for duplicating or publishing the member's work and help family historians find places (libraries, archives, and historical societies) to donate their findings. The club could even maintain a small library and invite guest speakers to address the members. Above all, a family-history club can offer fellowship to the individual historian, forming a community of those united by the same interests and objectives.

You can also join or begin a family association for people with a common ancestry. Each year the *Genealogical Helper* publishes a list of established associations, and you can see if you qualify for membership in any of them. A family association may embrace all those with a certain surname or it may include only those descended from a particular ancestor (the descendants of Jessie Smith). Restricted membership is, of course, necessary for common surnames like Smith, Brown, or Johnson. If you plan to found a new association, begin with your closest relatives. Elicit their active support for your project, then expand your efforts to include more distant members of the family.

A successful family association should offer encouragement for research and means for the sharing of information. It could publish a newsletter, circulate members' manuscripts, hold reunions and meetings, and maintain an archive of sources and written work. Membership in a family association brings the special satisfaction of expanding your knowledge while bringing you closer to those with whom you share the bond of a common heritage.

THE FULFILLMENT OF RESEARCH

Family historians find that recovery of the past is its own reward. You will not need to produce anything tangible to experience the exhilaration of discovery or the awareness that comes from going beyond the limits of personal recollection. Eli N. Evans, author of *The Provincials: A Personal History of Jews in the South,* recently wrote that his interest in family history began when he "chanced upon a yellowing typed manuscript . . . that my grandmother Jennie Nachamson had dictated to one of her eight daughters during the last year of her life in 1939. The story told of the early days in Lithuania, the family debate to come to America, the first few years in a Baltimore slum and subsequently of my grandparents' decision to gamble on the South." Evans's discovery led to years of research and to the writing of his acclaimed volume. Aside from his book, Evans found that doing family history was itself "one of the deepest and most fulfilling experiences in my life." Just talking with relatives about the family's past, he wrote, "made me feel less lonely somehow—no longer a particle of sand on the beach but part of all our family and the immigrant generation who went before and struggled, wandered, settled, loved, married, and bore children. Talking about our family history provided me not only a bridge to the past but an anchor for the future."

You may never write a book or even a composition about your own family. But you can still experience the fulfillment that Evans expressed. The more deeply you probe the family's past, the more you will find it becoming part of your own sense of who you are. As a family historian, you look backward in time, but you still come face to face with yourself.

Be prepared for findings that could change your life. One student actually met his father for the first time since early childhood when doing a class project in family history. Only after beginning to study his past and learning how to use records did he gain the motivation to become reunited with his father and the ability to trace his whereabouts. Another student found herself revising ideas about her ethnic heritage that she had held all of her life. She had always considered herself to be strictly of Irish descent. Upon exploring her family history, however, she learned that she was also Scotch, Welsh, and German.

But the results of your study need not all be so personal and intangible. The knowledge you gain can be passed on to your family as a legacy that endures indefinitely. Collectively the legacy of humankind includes the learning and wisdom preserved in books, the stories that are told by word of mouth, and the art and architecture that survives from one generation to the next. As individuals, a more personal legacy may bind us to our ancestry: a family farm, a home, a skill or profession, or an item handcrafted by an ancestor. But for many of us today, the legacy left by our forebears is a purely material one that offers little sense of continuity from past to present.

More than two thousand years ago, the Greek historian Thucydides eloquently explained how history becomes a legacy for future generations:

> The absence of romance in my history will, I fear, detract somewhat from its interest; but if it be judged useful by those inquirers who desire an exact knowledge of the past as an aid to the interpretation of the future, which in the course of human things must resemble it if it does not reflect

> it, I shall be content. In fine, I have written my work, not as an essay which is to win the applause of the moment, but as a possession for all time.

Within your own family, the historical research that you do can also become a "possession for all time." You offer to family members the gift of their own history, providing knowledge of a common past that has led to the present and points toward the future.

SELECTED BIBLIOGRAPHY

I. Scholarship in Family History

Ariès, Philippe, *Centuries of Childhood: A Social History of Family Life* (New York: Vintage Books, 1962) A classic survey of the European family from the Middle Ages to the seventeenth century; argues that modernization meant the triumph and not the eclipse of the family.

Chafe, William H., *The American Woman: Her Changing Social, Economic, and Political Roles, 1920–1970* (New York: Oxford University Press, 1972) A sound, factually based account.

Daedalus (Spring 1977), *The Family*. Special issue devoted to looking at the family from the perspectives of various disciplines.

Demos, John, *A Little Commonwealth: Family Life in Plymouth Colony* (Cambridge: Cambridge University Press, 1970) A suggestive study that combines psychological theory with research into literary and statistical sources.

Elder, Glen H., Jr., *Children of the Great Depression: Social Change in Life Experience* (Chicago: University of Chicago Press, 1974) A study of how economic depression affected the family life of those growing up in the 1930's.

Gordon, Michael, ed., *The American Family in Social-Historical Perspective* (New York: St. Martin's Press, 1973) An excellent collection of essays; the best introduction to American family history.

Greven, Philip J., Jr., *Four Generations: Population, Land, and Family in Colonial Andover, Massachusetts* (Ithaca: Cornell University Press, 1970) A demographic study that links family life to social and economic history.

Gutman, Herbert G., *The Black Family in Slavery and Freedom 1750–1925* (New York: Pantheon Books, 1976) The key work on the black family for the period covered; challenges the notion that slavery destroyed black family life.

Handlin, Oscar, *The Uprooted,* 2nd ed. (Boston, Little, Brown, 1973) First published in 1951, a seminal account of immigration to the United States.

Hunt, David, *Parents and Children in History: The Psychology of Family Life in Early Modern France* (New York: Basic Books, 1970) An insightful challenge to Ariès's interpretation of family history.

Lichtman, Allan J., and Joan R. Challinor, eds., *Kin and Communities in America* (forthcoming) Selections of material from the Smithsonian Institution's Sixth International Symposium on Kin and Communities, June 14–17, 1977.

Rabb, Theodore K., and Robert I. Rotberg, eds., *The Family in History: Interdisciplinary Essays* (New York: Harper & Row, 1971) A wide-ranging collection of essays taken primarily from a special issue of the *Journal of Interdisciplinary History.*

Russo, David J., *Families and Communities: A New View of American History* (Nashville: American Association for State and Local History, 1974) Explores possibilities for revising American history through a focus on family and local history.

Shorter, Edward, *The Making of the Modern Family* (New York: Basic Books, 1975) An extension of Ariès's thesis that relies heavily on statistical information.

Stack, Carol B., *All Our Kin* (New York: Harper & Row, 1974) Shows that family life may be founded neither on the household nor on conventional notions of kinship roles.

Thernstrom, Stephan, *Poverty and Progress: Social Mobility in a Nineteenth Century City* (Cambridge, Mass.: Harvard University Press, 1964) A pioneering study of social mobility in the United States.

Watts, Jim, and Allen F. Davis, *Generations: Your Family in Modern American History* (New York: Alfred A. Knopf, 1974) A collection of essays and commentary that combines personal and general history.

II. ORAL HISTORY

Banaka, William H., *Training in Depth Interviewing* (New York: Harper & Row, 1971) Especially useful for its annotated bibliography.

Baum, Willa K., *Oral History for the Local Historical Society*, 2nd ed. (Nashville, Tenn.: American Association for State and Local History, 1971) A brief and practical introduction for the beginner.

Dexter, Lewis Anthony, *Elite and Specialized Interviewing* (Evanston, Ill.: Northwestern University Press, 1970) Reflections on interviewing rather than a manual of techniques.

Gorden, Raymond L., *Interviewing: Strategy, Techniques, and Tactics* (Homewood, Ill.: Dorsey Press, 1975) A thoughtful treatise that is especially strong on the interview session.

Grele, Ronald J., ed., *Envelopes of Sound: Six Practitioners Discuss the Method, Theory and Practice of Oral History and Oral Testimony* (Chicago: Precedent Publishing Company, 1975) A discussion of philosophy, techniques, and interpretation.

Kramer, Sydelle, and Jenny Masur, *Jewish Grandmothers* (Boston: Beacon Press, 1975) Uses oral history for reconstructing individual and family experience.

Montell, William Cynwood, *The Saga of Coe Ridge: A Study in Oral History* (Knoxville, Tenn.: University of Tennessee Press, 1970) Uses oral history to reconstruct historical events in the absence of written records.

Moss, William W., *Oral History Program Manual* (New York: Praeger Publishers, 1974) How to set up a major project in oral history; includes twelve pointers useful to all oral historians.

Olch, Peter D., and Forrest C. Pogue, *Selections From the Fifth and Sixth National Colloquia on Oral History* (New York: Oral History Association, 1972).

Oral History Review. Published annually by the Oral History Association, New York.

Payne, Stanley L., *The Art of Asking Questions* (Princeton, N.J.:

Princeton University Press, 1951) Contains useful suggestions on the wording of questions.

Richardson, Stephen A., Barbara S. Dohrenwend, and David Klein, *Interviewing: Its Form and Functions* (New York: Basic Books, 1955) A thorough examination of interviewing procedure, primarily for social scientists.

Shumway, Gary L., and William G. Hartley, *An Oral History Primer* (Salt Lake City: Deseret Book Co., 1974) A brief guide for beginners.

Vansina, Jan, *Oral Tradition: A Study in Historical Methodology* (London: Routledge and Kegan Paul, 1965) The classic study on tapping people's oral traditions.

Waserman, Manfred J., comp., *Bibliography on Oral History* (New York: Oral History Association, 1975) An annotated bibliography of books and articles.

Zeitlin, Steven, et al., eds., *Family Folklore* (Washington, D.C.: Smithsonian Institution, 1976) Oral history, photographs, and other material from visitors to the Smithsonian Institution's Festival of American Folklife.

III. Home Sources and Photographs

Durant, Mary, *American Heritage Guide to Antiques* (New York: McGraw-Hill, 1970).

Felt, Thomas E., *Researching, Writing, and Publishing Local History* (Nashville, Tenn.: American Association for State and Local History, 1976) A guide for the neophyte in local history.

Green, Jonathan, ed., *The Snapshot* (Millerton, N.Y.: Aperture, 1974) Professional photographers writing about and showing their snapshots.

Lewis, Ralph H., *Manual for Museums* (Washington, D.C.: National Park Service, 1976) Includes useful information on caring for documents and objects.

Lieberman, Archie, *Farm Boy* (New York: Harry N. Abrams, 1974) Photographs of a farm family from 1950–1970; shows that you don't have to go back several generations to put together a family history.

Lynch, Kevin, *What Time Is This Place?* (Cambridge, Mass.: MIT Press, 1976) Learning from the environment.

Nelki, Andra, and Hilary and Mary Evans, *The Picture Researcher's Handbook* (New York: Charles Scribner's Sons, 1975).

Noren, Catherine Hanf, *The Camera of My Family* (New York: Alfred A. Knopf, 1976) The hundred-year history of a family told through the hundreds of photographs still in the family's possession.

Plenderleith, H. J., and A. E. A. Werner, *The Conservation of Antiquities and Works of Art: Treatment, Repair and Restoration,* 2nd ed. (London: Oxford University Press, 1971) A standard work in this field.

Simpson, Jeffrey, *The American Family: A History in Photographs* (New York: Viking Press, 1976) A photographic history of American families from the earliest days of photography to the 1970's.

Welling, William, *Collectors' Guide to Nineteenth-Century Photographs* (New York: Collier Books, 1976) An excellent guide to the identification of nineteenth-century photographs.

Weitzman, David, *Underfoot: An Everyday Guide to Exploring the American Past* (New York: Scribner's, 1976) A breezily written beginners' guide that touches upon photographs, objects, cemeteries, and buildings.

IV. GENEALOGY

American Genealogical Research Institute Staff, *How to Trace Your Family Tree* (Garden City, N.Y.: Doubleday, 1975) A competent and readable introduction to genealogical research.

American Society of Genealogists, *Genealogical Research: Methods and Sources,* 2 vols. (Washington, D.C., 1960, 1966) Along with brief discussions of genealogical methods and sources, these volumes explore research in particular states and countries.

Blockson, Charles L., with Ron Fry, *Black Genealogy* (Englewood Cliffs, N.J.: Prentice-Hall, 1977) A beginning survey of this field.

Colket, Meredith B., Jr., *Guide to Genealogical Records in the National Archives* (Washington, D.C.: Government Printing Office, 1964) Will be supplanted by Bill R. Linder and James D. Walker, *Guide to Genealogical Records in the National Archives* (forthcoming).

Doane, Gilbert H., *Searching for Your Ancestors: The How and Why of Genealogy*, 4th ed. (Minneapolis: University of Minnesota Press, 1973) First published in 1937, this is a classic introduction to genealogy.

Everton, George B., Sr., ed., *The Handy Book for Genealogists,* 6th ed. (Logan, Utah: Everton Publishers, 1971) A guide to state and county histories, maps, libraries and other genealogical resources.

Greenwood, Val D., *The Researcher's Guide to American Genealogy* (Baltimore: Genealogical Publishing Company, 1973) A detailed guide to genealogical techniques and resources. Excellent as a reference work.

Helmbold, F. Wilbur, *Tracing Your Ancestry: A Step-by-Step Guide to Researching Your Family History* (Birmingham, Ala.: Oxmoor House, 1976) A brief and elementary introduction to genealogical research and sources.

Jacobus, Donald Lines, *Genealogy as Pastime and Profession,* 2nd ed. (Baltimore: Genealogical Publishing Company, 1968) Essays by the late "Dean of American Genealogy."

Pine, Leslie G., *The Genealogist's Encyclopedia* (New York: Weybright and Talley, 1969) Includes information on research in most foreign countries.

Rottenberg, Dan, *Finding Our Fathers: A Guidebook to Jewish Genealogy* (New York: Random House, 1977) Notable for its list of surnames.

Stevenson, Noel C., ed., *The Genealogical Reader: A Collection of Articles Selected and Edited* (Salt Lake City: Deseret Book Co., 1958) A useful collection of articles on genealogical research.

Westin, Jeane Eddy, *Finding Your Roots: How Every American Can Trace His Ancestors—At Home and Abroad* (Los Angeles: J. P. Tarcher, 1977) An introduction to genealogy for beginners that briefly touches on many different topics.

Wright, Norman E., *Building an American Pedigree* (Provo, Utah: Brigham Young University Press, 1974) A long and detailed survey of genealogical source material. Excellent as a reference work.

V. HISTORICAL RESEARCH AND WRITING

Ashley, Paul P., *Say It Safely: Legal Limits in Publishing, Radio, and Television*, 4th ed. (Seattle: University of Washington Press, 1969) Discusses issues such as copyrighting, plagiarism, libel, and privacy.

Baker, Sheridan, *The Practical Stylist* (New York: Thomas Y. Crowell Co., 1962) A concise review of principles and rules for good writing.

Barzun, Jacques, and Henry F. Graff, *The Modern Researcher* (New York: Harcourt, Brace, 1970) The best traditional guide to researching and writing history.

Carter, Clarence E., *Historical Editing* (Washington, D.C.: National Archives, 1952) Useful for those compiling primary sources.

Fischer, David Hackett, *Historians' Fallacies: Toward a Logic of Historical Thought* (New York: Harper & Row, 1970) One historian's view of how his colleagues have gone wrong.

Lichtman, Allan J., and Valerie French, *Historians and the Living Past: The Theory and Practice of Historical Study* (Chicago: A.H.M. Publishers, 1978) Includes chapters on historical inference, explanation, research, and writing.

Modern Language Association of America, *The M.L.A. Style Sheet*, 2nd ed. (New York: Modern Language Association, 1970).

Shafer, R. J., *A Guide to Historical Method* (Homewood, Ill.: Dorsey Press, 1969) Straightforward, practical approach to the use of historical evidence.

Strunk, William Jr., and E. B. White, *The Elements of Style* (New York: Macmillan, 1972) Unerringly good advice for writers presented in less than one hundred pages.

Turabian, Kate L., *A Manual for Writers of Term Papers, Theses, and Dissertations,* 4th ed. (Chicago: University of Chicago Press, 1975) Explains the proper form to be used when writing a formal paper.

Winks, Robin W., ed., *The Historian as Detective: Essays on Evidence* (New York: Harper & Row, 1968) Entertaining and informative essays about how historians infer conclusions from their evidence.

Appendix

SAMPLE QUESTIONS FOR A MAIL QUESTIONNAIRE

Name____________________ Address ____________________
Date of birth______ Sex___ Place of birth: city __________
state__________ country____________________
If you were not born in the U.S., when did you move here? __
Are you a U.S. citizen?______
Religious preference__________ Racial background _________
Highest level of education____________________
Where were you born? at a hospital_____ at home_____ other
(please list) ____
Who supervised your birth? family doctor____ obstetrician____
midwife_____ relative_____ other (please list) ____________
What is your most vivid childhood memory? _______________
____

At what age did you first attend school?__________
Did you ever have to leave school for an extended period?_____
Why? ____
____

At what age did you first take a paying job?_____
What was the job? ____
What occupations have you had during your life? ___________
____

At what age did you begin dating?_____ What were dates like
when you were young? _____________________________________
____

What types of books, if any, did you read at home when you were a child? ______________________________

____

What type of reading was not allowed in the home? ______

____

Which of your parents and grandparents could read and write?

____

How were you disciplined as a child? ______________

____

How does your approach to child-rearing differ from that of your parents? ______________________________

____

List the people who resided in your household when you were a child.

father____ other relatives (please list)____
mother____ household help____
brother____ boarder____
sister____ other nonrelatives (please list)____
grandparent____

Do you remember using kin terms like "aunt" or "cousin" to describe nonrelatives? (please list) ______________
Were these people treated like members of the family? ______

____

At what age did you leave the home of your parents or guardians?____
Why did you leave? ______________________
How did you meet your spouse?______________________
Why did you get married when you did?______________
Who influenced your marital decision? ______________
About how many times did you move while still living with parents or guardians?____ How many of these moves were from one state to another or from one country to another?____
What were the major reasons for these moves? __________

____

About how many times have you moved since leaving the household of parent or guardian?____ How many of these moves

were from one state to another or from one country to another? ____ What were the major reasons for these moves? ________
____

How many children do you have? ____ When did you have your first child? ____________
List any languages other than English that are spoken in your household. ____________
List any languages other than English that were spoken in your household when you were a child. ____________
List the organizations and clubs to which you belong. ________
____
____

Do you attend church or another place of worship? ____
List the countries of any foreign relatives whom you have seen or corresponded with. ____________
Other than America, are there any countries you feel close to? ____ If yes, please list. ____________
Do you feel it is important to maintain the customs and traditions of your ancestors? very important ____ slightly important ____ not important ____
If you have immigrant ancestors, where did they come from (country and city or town if possible), approximately when did they arrive in America, and where did they first settle (city and state if possible)?
Mother's side ____________
____

Father's side ____________
____

Why do you believe your ancestors came to America? ____
____
____

Other than through marriage, have you or any of your ancestors ever changed your last name? ____ Original name ________
New name ________
Which if any of your ancestors or relatives are you named after? first name ____________ middle name ____________

Can you relate any stories about the history of your first or last name? ______________________________

____

Can you relate any other family stories that were passed on to you? ______________________________

____

What special sayings or expressions does your family have? __

____

What are their origins? ______________________________

____

What recipes or customs regarding food have been preserved in your family? ______________________________

____

How were they handed down? ______________________________

What family heirlooms do you possess? ______________________________

____

Why are they valuable to you? ______________________________

____

What is their history? ______________________________

____

Do you have any "black sheep" in the family? ______________________________

____

Why are they considered "black sheep"? ______________________________

____

Does your family hold reunions? _____ Where? ______________

When? ______________ How often? ______________

Who is invited? ______________________________

Who attends? ______________ Describe what goes on at a reunion. ______________________________

____

____

Have you or members of your family experienced racial, ethnic, religious, or sexual discrimination? _____ Please describe. ____

____

____

List and describe how local events have importantly affected your family life. ______________________________

Do you feel that your economic position is better than, worse than, or about the same as that of your parents or guardians?

____

What do you feel are the major differences between your current family and the family of your parents or guardians when you were a child? _______________

____

____

Have you ever been employed by a relative?_____ Have you ever employed a relative?_____ Have you ever borrowed money from a relative?_____ Have you ever lent money to a relative?_____ Have you ever participated in a partnership or other business venture with a relative?_____ Please describe these activities. _______________

____

____

Which, if any, of the following historical events do you believe importantly affected life within your family or within your parents' or guardians' family when you still lived with your parents or guardians? World War I_____ the depression of the 1930's _____ Franklin Roosevelt's New Deal_____ World War II_____ the Korean War_____ the civil rights movement of the 1960's _____ the women's liberation movement_____ Watergate_____
How did these events affect your family life? _______________

____

____

List the individuals currently residing in your household:

spouse_____	other relatives (please list) _______________
son_____	household help_____
daughter_____	roommate_____
mother_____	boarder_____
father_____	other nonrelatives (please list) _______________

Which of these relatives and nonrelatives would you regard as members of your immediate family? _______________
List any other relatives or nonrelatives who have lived in your household during the past five years. _______________

____

List the individuals who resided in your household when you were a child.

father_____ other relatives (please list) __________

mother_____ household help_____

brother_____ boarder_____

sister_____ other nonrelatives (please list) _______

grandparent_____

How often do you talk to or see relatives residing outside your household? every day_____ three to six days per week_____ one to two days per week_____ one to three days per month_____ less than one day per month_____

How often do you take your vacations with one or more members of your immediate family? always_____ mostly_____ rarely _____ never_____

How often does your other recreational activity include members of your immediate family? always_____ mostly_____ rarely _____ never_____

Do you rent or own your place of residence?_________

List any records or documents that you consulted in order to fill out this questionnaire. ______________________________

Please supply the following information about your spouse, or if divorced or widowed, your former or late spouse.

Date of birth________ Place of birth: city______________

state________ country_________________

If not born in the U.S., when did your spouse move here?____

Is your spouse a U.S. citizen?______

Religious preference_________ Racial background ________

Current occupation, or if unemployed, last occupation _____

Highest level of education_________________

If your spouse has immigrant ancestors, where did they come from (country and city or town if possible), and approximately when did they arrive in America and where did they first settle (city and state if possible)?

Mother's side____

____

Father's side ____

____

Please supply the following information for your parents and grandparents:

Mother:

Date of birth________ Place of birth: city____________
state________ country____________ If deceased, age at death and place of death ______________________________
____

Religious preference________ Racial background ________
Current occupation, or if unemployed, retired, or deceased, last occupation ______________________________________
Highest level of education______________ U.S. citizen?_____
Number of children_____
Your memories and impressions of your mother __________
____

Major events in her life ______________________________

Father:

Date of birth________ Place of birth: city____________
state________ country____________ If deceased, age and place of death ______________________________________
____

Religious preference________ Racial background ________
Current occupation, or if unemployed, retired, or deceased, last occupation ______________________________________
Highest level of education______________ U.S. citizen?_____
Number of children_____
Your memories and impressions __________________________
____

Major events in his life ______________________________

Maternal grandmother:

Date of birth________ Place of birth: city____________
state________ country____________ If deceased, age at death and place of death ______________________________
____

Religious preference________ Racial background ________
Current occupation, or if unemployed, retired, or deceased, last occupation ______________________________________

Highest level of education________________ U.S. citizen?_____
Number of children_____
Your memories and impressions ____________________________
____
Major events in her life ___________________________________

Maternal grandfather:
Date of birth__________ Place of birth: city______________
state_________ country______________ If deceased, age at death and place of death _____________________________________
____
Religious preference_________ Racial background __________
Current occupation, or if unemployed, retired, or deceased, last occupation ____
Highest level of education________________ U.S. citizen?_____
Number of children_____
Your memories and impressions ____________________________
____
Major events in his life ___________________________________

Paternal grandmother:
Date of birth__________ Place of birth: city______________
state_________ country______________ If deceased, age at death and place of death _____________________________________
____
Religious preference_________ Racial background __________
Current occupation, or if unemployed, retired, or deceased, last occupation ____
Highest level of education________________ U.S. citizen?_____
Number of children_____
Your memories and impressions ____________________________
____
Major events in her life ___________________________________

Paternal grandfather:
Date of birth__________ Place of birth: city______________
state_________ country______________ If deceased, age at death and place of death _____________________________________
____

Religious preference__________ Racial background __________
Current occupation, or if unemployed, retired, or deceased, last occupation ______________________________
Highest level of education________________ U.S. citizen?_____
Number of children_____
Your memories and impressions ______________________________
____
Major events in his life ______________________________

Please supply the same information requested for your parents and grandparents for any children you may have over the age of twenty-five. Please supply any information that you may have for ancestors earlier than your grandparents. Use additional sheets of paper if necessary.

INDEX

ABOUT THE AUTHOR

ALLAN J. LICHTMAN, associate professor of American history at The American University in Washington, D.C., has used family-history projects in many of his courses. As a consultant to the Smithsonian Institution's program on kin and communities, he directed a national symposium on family history and taught personal family history in the Smithsonian Associates Program. He was guest speaker at the University of California Conference on Family History and has published articles in the *Journal of Negro History*, the *Journal of Interdisciplinary History*, the *American Historical Review* and the *New Republic*. His other books include *Historians and the Living Past: The Theory and Practice of Historical Study* (with Valerie French), *Ecological Inference* (with Laura Irwin Langbein), and *Prejudice and the Old Politics: The Presidential Election of 1928* (forthcoming). He lives in Bethesda, Maryland.